I0560239

WELCOME TO THE STAGE

The 360° Approach to Hosting Events Like a Pro

Sara Deacon

RADEAC MEDIA

For more information, email sara@saradeacon.com

For the people in my network, who encourage me to be bold.
For the people in my community, who allow me to be real.
And for the people in my family, who love me no matter what.

Contents

Introduction

Welcome to the Stage

PLEASE TAKE YOUR SEATS

"Thoughts become things. If you see it in your mind, you will hold it in your hand."

— Bob Proctor

I MAGINE YOU'RE HOSTING YOUR next event. You've poured months into planning it, selecting top-notch speakers and wooing some incredible big-name sponsors. You're passionate about the topic, and you've managed to nail the marketing to your lists and followers in such a way that tickets have sold out! The venue is amazing, your production team is on point, and you know that this event will help your business grow by at least 5x over the next few hours.

The big day arrives, and you're fueled up with passion and caffeine. You set yourself up near the registration table with some of your favorite volunteers and begin greeting your guests as they arrive. They're buzzing with excitement and anticipation, and you can't wait to share your meticulously planned program with them. In fact, as they arrive, you can't stop yourself from sharing some stories with the attendees about how you secured that elusive speaker or had to replace the DJ at the last minute as folks are networking around you.

Someone starts telling you about how they almost couldn't make it because this crazy thing happened at their son's high school.

You assure them that it will all work out, and you tell them you're really glad they made it. In fact, you know the perfect person to introduce them to on the other side of the room who might be able to help them with their kid, and you're about to go introduce them when you glance at your smartwatch and see that the program should have started five minutes ago!

You haul ass to the main stage with a desperate glance at your production team, remembering that they still haven't mic'd you up, and by the time you take the stage, half of your audience is sitting in their seats checking their own watches and phones while the other half is still in the hallway obliviously conversing.

You clear your throat and try to breathe. What happened? This wasn't how you planned it. You're starting off behind and already thinking of ways to make up time. You clear your throat again and begin, "Ladies and gentlemen, please take your seats, it's time to begin."

And the conversations go on. And the people already seated stare at you expectantly.

Your heart beats faster and you repeat, "Please take your seats... please. Take your seats."

You forgot to plan for this.

Origin Story

Everything starts with a thought. You had the thought to use an event to grow your business, to raise money for your nonprofit or to celebrate and level up the top performers in your industry. Thoughts become things. You acted on your idea and created an event worth attending. I want to acknowledge you for this here at the start because most people are too scared to put themselves and their ideas out there at all.

My good friend and colleague Wendy Babcock did this very thing. And if it hadn't been for her thought and her thing, you wouldn't be holding this book. Wendy was looking to attend a specific type of women's event that blended the personal with the professional to empower herself as both a woman and as a business owner. She could not find this type of event anywhere, so in 2019, she created and hosted the very first *Warrior Unchained* event. It started with a thought about what one person needed for herself and her business, and it grew to take hold of others who recognized their need for the same thing.

In 2022, when she brought *Warrior* back after the pandemic, I was lucky enough to have a front row seat. I had been in business for myself prior to 2020, and like so many others, I had pivoted. I was focused on building a new business as a life coach, and I was interested in speaking in order to grow that business. I had very little idea what I was doing. What I did know was that surrounding myself with other people who knew different things than I did would be a good move. It was. As soon as I walked into the room, I knew that I was meant to be there.

The women in the audience were real and vulnerable with each other. The speakers shared personal stories of deep overcoming in both their lives and businesses. I absorbed practical and actionable wisdom from the stage that helped my business exactly where it was. It was a beautiful experience.

At the same time, there was something else I noticed as I sat at my table taking it all in. I noticed that Wendy was doing almost everything herself. Even though she had some volunteers helping to execute the production, she had her hands on every detail. I noticed the effort it took for her to keep all those plates spinning. I sensed her agitation and the strain of holding it all together.

After the event, I had a thought of my own. I thought about how that event had impacted me. I thought about making that kind of impact in my own life and business. I thought about the community that Wendy was curating through her work with female entrepreneurs, storytellers and speakers. I thought about what it might take to get me on stage at the next *Warrior Unchained* event.

In early 2023, as Wendy was planning her next conference and putting out her "call for speakers," I was still a complete novice at pitching myself. I knew I wanted to be part of what she was creating, so I began to brainstorm a talk to pitch that would fit. Before I could write or submit anything coherent, and before the deadline had even passed, all of the 2023 speakers had been selected.

I thought, "How can I get on that stage?"

I was lying on my living room floor in savasana at the end of one of my morning yoga practices when the thought that started me down my current path came to me. A mere two letters, the role had only recently begun to seep into my consciousness. M.C. Spelled out as "emcee," it stands for Master of Ceremonies, and I remembered how involved and overwhelmed Wendy had seemed handling all the things during her last event. She was host, emcee, event manager, keynote speaker, vendor coordinator, public relations, producer and more! I knew in my bones that having an emcee would take so much off her plate and help in countless other ways, and when I pictured myself in that very role, I felt the biggest YES I'd ever felt in my body in my whole life.

It started with a thought. The thought took hold and became a thing when I drafted an email to Wendy later that very day. I didn't know her very well at the time, and I was extremely nervous about how my thoughts might be received. I even scheduled the email to send a few days later, in case I chickened out! In the email, I complimented her event, sharing my appreciation for all of her efforts and my observation of the immense energy it took to do it all. Finally, I asked her if she had ever considered having an emcee. I asked, "What would it take for it to be me?"

When she received my email, the thought took hold of her, too. She had not considered using an emcee for her event, and she told me later that the thought of it lifted a heavy weight from her shoulders, leading to her enthusiastic YES! response. I took the stage as an emcee for the first time in September 2023 at the third *Warrior Unchained* women's business and empowerment conference.

From the moment I stepped up to the microphone on the opening night of the conference weekend, I knew I was meant to be there.

Since then, I have evolved away from coaching as a business. Even though I loved coaching, I realized that my zone of genius lies securely in the realm of audience engagement and activation as a speaker and emcee. In fact, I was awarded the Small Business Owners Community Speaker of the Year in 2024, proving to myself and others that the stage is where I truly belong.

Since Wendy gave me my first "big break," I have learned a lot about events as a business owner, speaker and emcee. I've also learned a lot about myself and about other humans. With this book, my intention is to share what I've learned in order to help you produce events that connect, inspire and engage long after the final round of applause.

When you find yourself wearing all the hats to produce your own event, you quickly learn how much is *really* involved in pulling off a successful experience for everyone in the room. The "emcee hat" is an incredibly fun one for the right person to wear. If that's you, in the pages that follow, I'm going to show you how to wear that hat with confidence, style and grace. If it's not, I'm still going to help you lead your event with confidence, and I'll guide you to making the right decision about who should master your ceremony when you're ready to hand it over. I'll offer some clear criteria for selecting the perfect emcee and show you how to maximize the return on your investment. Whether you're planning to DIY or delegate, this book will help you create memorable, professionally executed events that leave your audience wanting more.

Events can be incredible opportunities for entrepreneurs looking to grow their businesses. A great event or conference brings your ideal clients together and primes them to invest enthusiastically in your products and services. It cultivates long-lasting relationships between colleagues, associates and sponsors. It even has the potential to develop deep and lengthy friendships. *Warrior Unchained* was such an event for me, and my goal as an emcee is to elevate as many events as possible to a level of success that exceeds everyone's expectations.

You may not have the connections or resources to hire a professional emcee, and that's okay! When you understand and implement the strategies in this book, you'll call your audience to their seats with a clear, calm voice and a commanding stage presence that knocks their socks off every time!

Now, please take your seats so we can get started.

Part 1
WHY YOUR EVENT MATTERS

1
EVENTS GROW BUSINESSES

"People do not buy goods and services. They buy relations, stories and magic."

— Seth Godin

W HEN I WALKED INTO the room at the second *Cre8tive Con* event in Chicago, IL in February of 2025, I recognized my people. The hosts of this event gather creative entrepreneurs from all over the country (and Canada) to share new ways of doing business and introduce them to other creative people so they can leverage those connections and take their business further than they thought possible.

As I networked and learned, I saw my own experiences reflected in many of the others' stories. Creative entrepreneurs aren't like other business owners, and doing business as a creative can often feel lonely and isolating. Many times over the course of building my business, I've felt like I was the only one struggling to analyze my data or build and implement a marketing strategy.

In a room full of people like me, who have a thousand ideas a day and at least a hundred good ones, I felt at home. Among my fellow creatives, I saw that I was not alone in my struggles, and there were paths to success to be found in the stories surrounding me, which gave me hope and direction.

Events With Intention

What do you want your audience to learn? To know? To feel?

Think about the last event that had a profound impact on you. What was it about the event itself that made a difference? Was it the venue? Was it a specific speaker? Was it someone who sat at your table? A workshop that gave you concrete actions to implement? Was it a conversation you had in the hallway or over lunch? A story you can't get out of your head?

There are so many different kinds of events, each with their own nuances around the most effective way to host. Some entrepreneurs prefer small, intimate workshops, retreats or VIP days. Other businesses prefer to go big, hosting multi-day conferences, extravagant galas or 1000-guest fundraisers.

Regardless of the scale, events are good for business. They bring the right people into the right room at the right time and turn them into profitable partners, generous donors, long-term clients and raving fans. As the host, you're the center of the action. All eyes are on you. Your ROI should be the largest in the room, even if it doesn't exactly take the form of dollars you can count.

As the host, you are the thought leader, authority, connector, activator and expert. In order to see the return on your investment of time and resources, you want to put your best face forward. Most event hosts think that this means being on stage as much as possible. However, as you'll learn in the following pages, there are times when more credibility comes from the way other people present and perceive you and your brand than what comes out of your own mouth.

I'm going to show you how to host your event like a professional so that you look good, your speakers look good, and your sponsors and guests can't wait to participate in whatever you invite them to next. The concepts we'll discuss can apply to many different types of events, and when you develop some of these hosting skills, you'll likely find ways to apply them to your day-to-day interactions as well.

I'm well aware that as the producer and host of your event, whatever it may be, you'll be wearing at least 20 different hats throughout the preparation, execution and follow-up phases. When you are able to keep your vision in mind and focus on why you're creating the kind of event you're creating, you'll more clearly see the impact of the event on your bottom line.

As both an emcee and an attendee, I've seen where a lack of focus has led to missed opportunities. I've also witnessed an event host sell out of their next program because of how brilliantly they communicated their vision of their event. I'm sure that you'd prefer to experience the latter, so let's explore some different ways to focus for maximum success.

2

FIVE WAYS TO FOCUS

"The successful warrior is the average person, with laser-like focus."

— Bruce Lee

T HINK ABOUT THE LAST event you attended. Why did you go? What was the theme of the event? What were the learning objectives? What kind of people were in the room? Who were the sponsors? And what do you remember the most?

Often, the reason you host an event and the reason someone attends it are not the same. Hold this thought as we consider some different ways to focus your event.

Because I'm a word nerd with an appreciation for alliteration, we're going to discuss five "C's" that events tend to have as main goals: Cash, Credibility, Clients, Community and Collaboration.

Most events serve multiple purposes, and you may resonate with all five of these reasons for hosting your event. My invitation to you would be to rewrite this list in order of your priorities for your event and organization.

Cash

It's 100% okay to admit that you are building out an event in order to make money. I would bet that most entrepreneurs who host an event are expecting to make a profit. Even if you don't say this part to anyone else, search your soul, and you'll probably find a seed of hope that you're going to make a bunch of money as a result of bringing people together.

I wanted to start by discussing the income goal. When you're running a business or organization, you're constantly concerned with your bottom line. Hosting an event requires a certain level of investment and risk, so admitting that you want to make money with your event is really, really smart. The desire to generate revenue from the event is going to be part of all of the other reasons for hosting an event, whether you realize it or not, so let's go ahead and say the quiet part out loud and dive right into a discussion about cold hard cash.

In order to turn a profit on an event, your main focus must be on the numbers. You'll need to keep costs low and focus on spon-sorships and ticket sales. You might consider offering pay-to-play speaking spots on your stage for those who are eager to get in front of your audience. This is a type of sponsorship where speakers give an educational, value-packed talk or workshop and make an offer or invitation to the audience. This generates leads for their own product or service at your event, and they pay you for the opportunity to do it.

When your primary objective is money, treat your event like its own "mini-business." You may even want to create a mini business plan and set a strict budget for it, enlisting others to help if you're like me and don't always play nice with numbers.

WATCH OUT!

I've spoken with many event hosts who have lost money on events they expected to profit from because they failed to consider the obvious and not-so-obvious money leaks!

If your focus is cash, your budget is not a suggestion! Most event hosts quickly realize that it takes a lot more money than they think it does to host a pro-level event. Venue fees can get out of control fast, especially if you include food service, multiple spaces, the venue's tech services or other required add-ons. Read your contracts carefully!

If you plan to bring in celebrity keynote speakers, their fees can rapidly eat your budget, too, leading to the need for larger sponsorships or higher ticket prices.

Most entrepreneurs understand that earning income from events on their own can be a challenge, which is why you're likely to combine your focus on cash with another deeper or wider vision.

What kind of cash return do you expect from your event?

Credibility

A huge reason why someone might choose to attend an event is because of the name on the invitation. Maybe it's a celebrity name, or maybe the person attached to the event is an expert in something that people want to learn.

You have a personal brand, and if you own your own business, both your personal and business brand identities are deeply entwined.

Hosting an event provides brand visibility and credibility for several reasons.

When you're at the helm of your event, you're the go-to for information about the event itself as well as how to connect with the speakers or presenters you bring to your stage. You get multiple opportunities to share who you are and what you do with others, which begins from the moment you start marketing your event. As you promote what you're creating and building and how you're bringing people together, even people who don't plan to attend your event will notice what you're doing, who you're doing it for and how you're positioning your brand and your expertise in order to deliver the experience you promise.

Even if you've never hosted an event before or you're in the early phases of building your business, positioning yourself as a thought leader by bringing yourself to the center of your own stage makes you the go-to for all things related to the topic or theme of your event. People will be drawn to you before, during and after the event and think of you when they are looking for the products or services you offer in your business.

When your main focus is on building your credibility, your short term ROI might not be ideal. You might even lose money on the event itself and have to treat it as a marketing investment, gathering people together to share your differentiators with them so that they can get to know, like and trust you. When you speak with authority about what you've built, you set yourself up to receive invitations to speak, consult or collaborate with other organizations or event hosts long-term. This generally leads to more revenue than what you could make from an event produced for the purpose of generating cash from ticket sales and sponsorships alone.

WATCH OUT!

I've attended events that were so focused on the host's own credibility and brand positioning that they failed to account for the real needs of their audience.

Even though your goal is to showcase your own expertise, no one wants to hear you brag the whole time or be constantly sold to. Be careful that the whole event isn't the YOU show. Share the stage with people you've vetted, who align with your message and add insane amounts of value to your audience. Show up to serve them, and you will indeed shine. Find the balance between building your credibility and stroking your ego.

When you create a memorable experience for your guests, they'll keep talking about you, your business and your event. When other people recommend you, it's even more impactful than when you go around tooting your own horn.

How can your event boost your credibility or that of your brand?

Clients

I can't count how many times I've been told by marketing experts to show up where my clients hang out in order to generate warm leads. If you're like me, though, you can only be in one physical location at a time and only have 24 hours in a day. So why not bring your ideal clients to you?

What problem does your business solve? Who has that problem? What's an experience that you can offer to them that will bring them closer to your solution?

Many hosts develop their events with the intention to gather leads together and turn them into paying clients. Market your event in a way that it becomes a no-brainer decision for your leads to attend. As they experience your event, you're educating them and qualifying them to work with you. You're offering massive value for your potential clients as well as for the people who may never buy from you (though they could become great referral partners as a result of your generosity in sharing your expertise). Your event's programming should help them solve a current problem and give them an easy win.

From there, reveal the gaps between the current problem's solution and their ability to solve the next one, which is ideally where your product or service comes in. Guide them through the process of taking a step closer to you by giving them an incredible experience of working with you, which leads them to becoming an enthusiastic supporter and a potential long-term client.

WATCH OUT!

Creating clients is all about trust!
You need to find the balance between giving real, tangible solutions in your content and leaving them wanting more. People are getting better every day at calling out the bullshit. You can't stay at surface level anymore because folks are more discerning about where they spend their time and their money. They're showing up expecting practical tools or transformation. Don't let them down.

If you're not sure how to hold this balance, hire a coach or con-sultant who will help you craft your messaging and train you to make offers from the stage without sounding too "salesy."

I've seen hosts sell out their programs by leveraging their events this way, giving massive value and building trust and relationships with their audiences and guests. I've also attended events that felt all about making the sale, giving little more than surface-level platitudes presented as solutions, which were not at all helpful in a practical way. The former are far more engaging and memorable for all the right reasons. Again, if the event itself only breaks even or loses money, qualifying and gathering people who need what you offer and are ready to buy can provide an exponential long-term ROI for your business.

What is the most common question you get from potential clients?

Community

Most of the time, when I am attending events, and even when I'm emceeing, my goal is to form a deep connection with someone in the room. I love meeting everyone, of course, and there's usually that *one* person I'll come home and tell my family about. It's the person I make a point to reach out to and set up a coffee date with afterwards, the person I can hardly believe I'm fortunate enough to count among my friends after a profound conversation with them at an event.

I've seen the title "Community Builder" on a number of LinkedIn pages recently. This tells me that community has become a pri-mary focus for businesses, both big and small, which makes sense post pandemic. In 2020, it became glaringly obvious how much being in community with other people improves our health and well-being. When we lost our communities, we collective-ly struggled. Providing clients, connections and collaborators with a sense of community establishes another layer of trust with your business and brand.

People are wired to look for belonging. Back in prehistoric times, if you didn't belong to a tribe or group, you literally would not survive. In business, giving your audience a sense of belonging and collective ownership of your mission, vision and values strengthens their bond with you and turns them into raving fans. Your community wants to see you succeed as much as you do, and when you're providing them with the connection and security of belonging to something bigger than themselves, they will do what they can to help you.

WATCH OUT!

While a sense of community is a good thing, it's easy for people to insulate themselves and reject people or ideas that at first don't seem to belong.
Create a safe place for the exploration of your event's broad-er vision, values or purpose while remaining open to things that challenge what you think you know about fitting in. Expression is important, and you want to make sure that you are allowing variation within your boundaries. If you create another echo chamber, you'll shut down the kind of discourse that encourages growth. We get enough of this kind of bias reinforcement and tribalism on social media. People are coming to you in person on purpose in part so they can step away from that sort of thing for a while.

It's an incredible feeling when you walk into a room knowing that the people around you are looking out for you, genuinely interested in helping you grow and want to see you succeed. Whether you're bringing people together to raise money for a worthy cause, learning something that will take people to a new level or celebrating accomplishments, everyone in the room is an important part of your event. It's your job to make them feel seen, heard and welcome in that space.

What's one thing that helps you feel connected with a group of people?

Collaboration

My friend Kim Knaak of Opportunity's Knaaking[1] uses the hashtag #collaborationnotcompetition. She moves through her life and business with collaboration as her top priority. I love attending events with Kim in the room because she practices what she preaches. She connects people with each other because she has experienced the value in building relationships with other people in business. She always puts people first—some might say too much— and she has grown her business while helping countless others to grow their own. Her tireless efforts bring people together and encourage them to work with each other, even when they appear to be competitors in the same business or market.

Events that emphasize collaboration are the most fun for me to attend and facilitate. Many business owners are turned off by "networking" when the people in the room treat it as a sales frenzy free-for-all, stabbing their business cards at as many people as possible and taking up all the time in a 1-on-1 meeting pitching you

---

1. https://opportunitysknaaking.com

their products and services. I don't go to those kinds of networking events anymore, and neither should you.

When we are networking or attending conferences or events, our goal should be to build relationships. Most of the time, you're not going to find a client at a networking event, conference or gathering of your peers. Instead, what usually happens is that you end up doing business *through* the people in those rooms instead of directly with them. In other words, look at the people in the room as your unofficial marketing team. They're going to be the ones talking about you to the people they know who need what you have to offer.

If networking is a dirty word to you, you can call this level of relationship building whatever you want. Kim calls it collaboration, Tad Hargrave with Marketing for Hippies calls it "Hub Marketing," and I've heard others talk about nurturing "Power Partnerships." Whatever you call it, the point is that you're cultivating strong, cooperative relationships with people.

Hosting an event that highlights collaboration might look like a health coach organizing a conference that brings complementary service professionals together to explore different ways to support clients' health journeys. In this example, the event might be sponsored by a local health food store or supplement shop and invite acupuncturists, energy workers and herbalists to speak. There could be vendor tables for chiropractors, massage therapists, reiki practitioners, nutritionists, personal trainers or physical therapists. In this kind of space, you can encourage everyone to learn about each other, explore ways to work together, refer to each other or collaborate in exciting new ways.

WATCH OUT!

If your true intention is to emphasize collaboration, leave the sales pitch at home!

Not everyone in business is used to operating from a position of genuine collaboration, so make sure to clearly and consistently communicate your collaborative intentions to your speakers, sponsors, vendors and guests.

Encourage group problem solving. Highlight others' strengths. Give more than you expect to receive. Don't hold back. Model this posture for your audience. Be intentional about who you invite to the stage and who you welcome into the room. Manage expectations. If people are coming to your event expecting to get clients, you've missed the mark, and you're not going to develop the kind of collaborative relationships you say you want.

Collaboration, credibility and community often go hand in hand, and your ability to bring people together and facilitate experiences and relationships is going to be tested. The ROI for collaboration events can truly be exponential when you nurture these partnerships throughout your career.

How did you meet your most important power partners?

Decision Time

Now that we've discussed five ways to focus your event, consider where your event falls?

- Are you most interested in generating cashflow from the events themselves?

- Are you looking to establish yourself as a thought leader and amplify your credibility in your field?

- Are you creating a lead funnel event to bring in more ideal clients?

- Are you establishing a community where people connect with each other and find value in belonging?

- Are you looking for fresh perspectives and new ways to collaborate and partner with others?

What is your event's top priority?

3
THE EMCEE EFFECT

"Your audience gives you everything you need. They tell you. There is no director who can direct you like an audience."

— Fanny Brice

I'VE BEEN TO A number of events that used an insider emcee instead of hiring an outside professional, where a member of the board or hosting company takes charge of the microphone. The pros of this approach include their ability to bring deep passion and connection to the cause. The cons include carrying other responsibilities beyond the scope of their role as emcee.

For example, I attended a conference that was hosted by two of the keynote speakers. As an audience member, when one of them took the stage to give their talk, I assumed that they were about to introduce someone else, which made it difficult to engage with their presentation until they were already well into it. As a result, the flow was off, and I felt unsettled.

In contrast, when I have attended events with a clear and separate emcee, I always know that when someone else takes the stage, they're going to present relevant content. Having one emcee who is not also a speaker or sponsor is often more effective and provides your audience with a cohesive experience throughout.

To align your event with any of the primary objectives we went over in the last chapter, the number one thing to keep in mind is consistency. Think of a time when the reality of a situation, product or service turned out differently than you expected. Take online shopping, for example. You can search plenty of social media posts that compare "What I ordered," to "What I got." It's funny when it's happening to other people about frivolous things like fast fashion online. It's not so funny when that's the feeling people are walking away with after an event that you poured your heart and soul into.

The number one way to achieve consistency in the flow and feel of your event is to give control of the microphone to someone who knows what to do with it. An emcee is more than a reader of speaker introductions and recognizer of sponsors. Your emcee is the first face of your event. They're the welcome wagon. They're a consistent presence that sets the stage to prepare your audience to learn from and engage with you. They are the primary communication channel for everyone involved with your event.

If you're thinking about stepping into the role of emcee for your own event, get ready to play the extrovert, even if that's not your natural tendency. You need to talk with people off stage, on stage and back stage. You need to know the names and faces of your VIPs and how to make them feel like the VIPs they are. You need to know how to pronounce the names of the people and the businesses involved in the experience. Your energy must be high, and your enthusiasm must be contagious.

The emcee effect is one of consistency. The emcee acts as a conduit between you and your audience as well as between your audience and the speakers, sponsors and other vendors present at your event. The emcee knows who you should know and why. The emcee knows why you're hosting your event, why people are attending and makes sure that the focus and flow of the event matches both.

Think about which of the five different areas is the main focus for your event (cash, credibility, clients, community, collaboration). From there, you can develop a theme, create a more specific vision or set a certain fundraising goal. As the event's producer, you have plenty of other things you're thinking about throughout the planning, preparation and production, too. Things like ticket sales, sponsor packages, educational materials, speaker spots, brand alignment, marketing and promotion, celebrity endorsements, contracts, venue specs, tech teams and more.

Consistency of experience demands that you put the people themselves at the top of your priority list. "UX" is a term that tech companies use to refer to the "user experience." It applies here, too. If you forget to factor in the people involved in these areas, your event will fall flat, you'll fall short of your goals and end up forgotten or worse in a matter of moments. People don't care how much you know or do until they know how much you care.[1] And they can't just know it. They need to feel it, too. Failing to care about the people helping your event succeed can put your whole operation at risk.

Emcee: Maker or Breaker of Events

As an emcee, I can assure you that my role goes much deeper than reading a script. A lot of hosts think, "How hard can it be to make announcements, introduce speakers, say the sponsors' names and fill some silence here and there?" This leads to haphazard emceeing and disappointing audience experiences. The emcee

---

1. "People don't really care how much you know—until they know how much you care"
   — Zig Ziglar

role is more strategic and impactful than hosts may realize, and it may not be until you experience the difference that you fully understand. That's okay. That's why I wrote this book.

A skilled professional emcee elevates an event. We bring coherence, energy and an added level of polish to the experience. While you certainly can, and sometimes must, emcee your own event or bring in an unsuspecting volunteer, there are hidden risks to doing it that way.

For example, companies who sponsor your event are going to expect a certain return on their investment with you. They want to be associated with a high level of professionalism in the execution of the event. They want your event to look good and run smoothly so that they look good for being a part of it. They may want to experience a level of luxury or extravagance. Small mistakes on stage can lead to big losses when it comes to sponsorships. Fellow emcee and speaker, Quinn Conyers, shared how a large event sponsor who had supported an event for five years didn't come back for a sixth because their name was mispronounced, their bio was ignored and their hype video was forgotten. These small mistakes were a big deal to a five-figure investor, and the event host paid the price.

It should come as no surprise that the key metrics influenced by a quality emcee have to do with their connection with the crowd. Remember, people are your number one focus, even when your primary goal involves bringing in a lot of cash!

You're hosting this event for a reason, and in order for your vision to come to fruition, everyone involved needs to get on board with it. Each person will be walking into that room with a different connection to your cause and their own unique reason for being there and getting involved. The collaborative relationship between emcee and host ensures that no matter how different they may be from each other when they come in, the people in the room leave with a real connection to you and, more importantly, to each other.

Quality emceeing engages the audience and inspires them to accept your future invitations with enthusiasm. Your emcee should enhance and elevate the performances of your keynote and breakout speakers. The emcee is often the one recognizing and encouraging appreciation for sponsors and success partners, making them feel more than satisfied with their level of investment in your occasion. And finally, the pacing, energy and flow of the event hinges on the emcee's ability to read the room and redirect without fracturing the audience's attention.

The 360° Approach

As I stood on the stage after the final speaker at the *Warrior Unchained* women's business and empowerment conference in southeastern Wisconsin in 2023, I could feel the weight of the weekend in the room like a collective held breath. The next item on the schedule was a panel with the full lineup of event speakers to close out our three-day experience.

I spoke some words to reinforce the previous speaker's message, and I was about to introduce the panel when I paused. I noticed and felt the energy of the room, recognized a need for a shift in the programming and decided to take a risk.

Instead of moving immediately into the next thing on the agenda, which was the panel discussion, I invited the audience to take a breath with me and soak in all of the learning and connections that they'd experienced over the past two days. I could feel their need to express and share some of those experiences, so I stepped off the stage and into the audience, with a glance at the event's host to make sure she trusted me enough to go off script.

I invited the audience members to share one thought or comment about the weekend. One person raised her hand and spoke. Then another one. Followed by someone else. We laughed, we cried and we connected. They encouraged each other, and they participated in a way they didn't think they would when they first bought their tickets to attend.

To this day, the event host still talks about how this was her favorite moment of the conference.

With a little bit of awareness and the courage to follow your instincts, you can create space for memorable moments like this at your event, too, without it feeling overly scripted or forced.

I call myself the 360° Emcee because I approach events from all angles—starting before, continuing during and extending after. I consider myself a connector, partner and collaborator from preparation to post production. I notice and address potential pitfalls before the host is even aware of them, and I make sure that everyone involved owns their roles. I'm constantly checking in on the energy of a room and looking for ways to make sure that the experience exceeds people's expectations.

There is art to this ability of an emcee to "read the room," and while you may be focusing on the big picture and handling the logistics and details behind the scenes, your emcee is monitoring audience energy and engagement, making adjustments and ad-libbing in order to keep things moving and maintain momentum. In between speakers, the emcee has an opportunity to reinforce the previous message and weave it into the next topic, seamlessly connecting one to another to amplify your event's theme and protect the emotional journey that you've designed. The emcee is also responsible for highlighting sponsors and success partners, showing genuine appreciation and encouraging the audience to get to know them better.

Some of these responsibilities might seem intangible, but together they create coherence and consistency, which makes your event feel intentional, on purpose and on brand instead of a scattered array of really cool separate segments.

Don't Wait Until It's Too Late

When planning events, a lot of hosts enlist an emcee's help as an afterthought. Unfortunately, as your event gets closer, the emcee has less time to collaborate with you and help you create the kind of experience you want for your guests. Emcees have a lot of value to add to your event, and when you don't realize you need an emcee until the last minute, the shortened timeframe for proper preparation will impact their performance. If you're not going to do it yourself, give yourself enough time to find an emcee that fits your vision, whether it's a team member, volunteer or a professional.

Look for an emcee who can challenge what you think you know about running an event. Look for someone who is not afraid to take charge but won't steal the spotlight. Look for someone who loves people. Look for someone well connected, who can make introductions to potential speakers and sponsors early on. Look for someone who is not afraid of feedback. Look for someone who is flexible and fun.

Your choice for your conference or convention emcee should not be an afterthought. It's probably not the greatest idea to assign the role to the first person who raises their hand and seems comfortable enough speaking in public. Whether you plan to step into the role yourself or delegate it, be intentional with your choice.

4

DREAM BIG, DELIVER BIGGER

"If your dreams don't scare you, they are too small."
— Richard Branson

L IKE THOUSANDS OF OTHER event hosts around the world, you want to make a difference. You want to inspire people to change their lives for the better. You might have a crystal-clear idea of how and why, or you might be at the beginning phases of ideation. I was asked in a recent interview, "What's your dream event?"

Let me ask you the same thing.

What's your dream event?

What kind of event do you want to create that *no one else can?*

Now that you've thought through some of the practical reasons why you want to host your event, it's time to dream. What's the ideal outcome? Who absolutely must be in the room in order to make it a success? What do you want to learn? What do you want to share? What do you want your audience to say as they're walking out the door?

If you knew you couldn't fail, what kind of experience would you create?

We've already discussed the different ways that events can help grow your business. A good event gathers your ideal clients, connections or collaborators together and primes them to refer to or invest in your business in a way that feels exciting and aligned.

A successful event offers opportunities well beyond the immediate thrill of sales or funds raised. A successful event cultivates long-lasting relationships between colleagues, associates and sponsors, and it can even be a catalyst for deep and lengthy friendships.

Once you envision and communicate your dream event, it's time to take deliberate action. It's about more than goals—it's about emotion. What do you want your audience to *feel* as you move them through your agenda?

Imagine the testimonial videos and surveys pouring in during the days that follow your wildly successful event. What are people saying?

Capture the Vision

Take some time to write a description of your dream event. Use these prompts or get out a blank page and start freewriting without self-judgment.

- Create a wish list of ideal speakers, guests, vendors and sponsors.

- What kind of transformations do you want people to experience during their time with each other and with you?

- What moments will your guests still be talking about six months later?

- How would you like to see your business or mission change

as a result?

- How do YOU want to show up?

Thoughts become things. When you write out your thoughts, you give them a greater chance of becoming real.

Now that you've put the dream down on paper, it's time to bring it to life. The best events are coherent and purposeful. Like any good story, they have a beginning, a middle and an end. The idea is to take your guests with you on a transformational journey.

THE BEGINNING:

How do you welcome your guests?

How do you set expectations and build anticipation? How do you make each person feel like the VIP that they truly are from the moment they walk in the door?

THE MIDDLE:

How do you facilitate connection?

How do you encourage engagement?

How do you build momentum and maintain energy throughout your event?

What do your guests learn and how will they apply it?

What opportunities for connection between attendees do you provide?

THE END:

How do your guests integrate their learning?

How do you lead your guests to take action?

How do you reinforce your core message and create a memorable finale?

How do you gather feedback?

How do you stay connected and top-of-mind in the days, weeks and months that follow?

I've witnessed event hosts sell out their programs and memberships because they designed their events with thoughtful intention. Each element served the individuals in ways that exceeded all of their expectations so that when they made their final offer or invitation, people could not sign up fast enough!

Room for Magic

The most successful events are the ones that plan well and at the same time do not have too rigid an attachment to the plans. As an emcee, I often experience the most powerful moments when things are *not* going according to plan. When you're willing to go off script and meet the audience where they are, magic happens.

The balance between structure and spontaneity offers the flexibility to adapt while maintaining the stability and consistency of your event's purpose.

As we move into Part 2, we'll explore how to execute your event's vision through skilled emceeing. Dreaming big and delivering bigger isn't about excessive planning or huge budgets, it's about being intentional when designing your event and mastering the basics of facilitation, communication and connection.

I'm going to give you everything I know about building confidence, commanding a room and creating the kind of seamless experiences that get standing ovations.

Before we get there, spend one more moment with your dream event. Visualize it in as much detail as possible. What does the room look like? How is the stage decorated? What do guests hear as they walk in? What's the energy like? How does the energy shift, ebb and flow through the course of the event?

What are people saying to each other in the parking lot as they avoid accepting that *their favorite event of all time* has come to an end?

The more vividly you can picture it, the more effectively you can bring your dream event to life!

Part 2

THE MAKING OF A GREAT EVENT

5

CRITICAL COMPONENTS

"Whatever you do, do it well. Do it so well that when people see you do it they will want to come back and see you do it again, and they will want to bring others and show them how well you do what you do."

— Walt Disney

I 'VE BEEN TO SOME incredible events. In fact, I consider myself completely and utterly spoiled by the first few events I attended as an entrepreneur because they were so exceptionally well done. I also formed some incredible relationships with some high quality people as a result. The *Small Business Owners Community*[1] annual conference is one I will never miss. The learning is top notch, the people are genuinely interested in helping each other out, and the production value is off the charts. The speakers are always brilliant and open to connecting, and the host, Pat Miller, shows up with professionalism, humility and deep, authentic gratitude for the community he has created.

---

1. https://smallbusinesscommunity.com

Warrior Unchained[2] events have a much different flavor. I love what we do with Warrior—how Wendy gets to the heart of the emotional and personal aspects of doing business as women. I love the dance parties and the silly videos. There are vendor tables and raffles to encourage speakers, sponsors and attendees to get to know each other, give and receive value. Like the SBOC conference, the caliber of speakers is extremely high, as is the quality of people gathered together in the audience.

Because these were among the first conferences I attended as an entrepreneur, I can't keep myself from noticing and comparing the differences between these events and the others I attend. There's nothing good or bad about these differences. Each event must embrace its own distinct energy that reflects its host or the host organization.

This is why the work we did in the last section is so important. You need to identify what makes a great event to YOU and determine your own definition of success.

Think again about a recent event or conference that you attended. What did it do well? Where did it fall short?

As someone who produces their own events, you're probably like me and attend events with a different perspective than the average ticket holder. I'm always experiencing events through the lens of an emcee, watching for techniques that might help elevate my own skill or for new ideas to offer to the hosts I work with. I'm also watching how the emcee navigates the flow of the event, whether they are part of the hosting organization or an outside professional. I'm keenly aware of spots where an emcee misses the mark or fails to appropriately transition or read the room.

---

2. The same event is now known as Legendary Women in Business (legendarywib.com).

In my humble opinion, the emcee gives an event its "wow factor."

What Does MC Stand For?

In the realm of events, the acronym MC means Master of Ceremonies. In rap/hip hop, MC stands for Microphone Controller, which feels pretty accurate to me, too. When I have control of the microphone, I get to do what I want because I've built trust and rapport with the host or organization who's hired me. Things often change between preparation for an event and the in-the-moment event experience, so you want someone on the microphone who can stay in control and ultimately continue to serve the event's mission.

Whether you intend to hand over complete control to an outside emcee or not, you must understand that the person in control of that microphone is going to be the one calling the shots. Choose your microphone controller or master of ceremonies wisely. Volunteering or "volun-telling" someone to be the face of your event, who doesn't know their way around a microphone, could lead to a number of mishaps that paint you and your occasion as unprofessional, scattered or boring. Trust me, you don't want that. Just because "Bob from accounting" might crack up the board members with his dad jokes about bookkeeping doesn't mean he's the best choice for a client-facing gala or company-wide recognition ceremony. When you're trying to bring in high-ticket sponsors and build lucrative relationships with strategic partners,

"Bob" might not be the best choice, no matter how willing or eager he might be to emcee.

I like to compare my role as an emcee to that of a nice rug—it really ties the room together. The right rug connects all the furniture and design elements in a space, and a good emcee brings all aspects of your event together for a cohesive experience.

I know it might come as quite a shock that I was a "theater kid" in high school and college. I loved acting, performing and being on stage. The only reason I didn't pursue professional acting was because I had other interests that took time away from perfecting the craft. I also knew that my talent alone wouldn't get me far at that level. Even though I didn't have the drive and determination to pursue an acting career, I learned a lot from my experiences performing at school, in clubs and for my local community theater.

One lesson that applies here is the importance of the stage crew. I've participated in productions both on stage and behind-the-scenes, and I can tell you that there is no way that a play, musical or any performance can be successful without a good crew. When I think about the role of the emcee, even though it is an on-stage role, it serves a purpose very similar to the stage crew.

The audience generally isn't there to see the emcee. I've come to terms with this fact, and I don't shed too many tears over it anymore, so you don't have to feel bad for me. Of course the audience is attending an event to learn from the speakers, to get close to the host or to make connections with the VIPs. Audiences are selfish like that. That being said, what happens to your conference experience when the emcee is obviously drunk? What happens in the theater when the curtain doesn't go up or comes down in the middle of a scene? You're pulled out of the moment and the value you get from the entire production goes down.

When you go to see a play, you're not there to see how well your favorite crew member moves the furniture or handles the curtains. When the stage crew does their job well, from your seat in the audience, you never notice their existence. You barely give them a thought because they blend so seamlessly in with the show that your focus remains on the story, the production and the actors doing their thing on stage.

When an emcee is on stage controlling the microphone and expertly directing the flow of the event, you might laugh at their jokes and put your hands in the air when they prompt you to wave them like you just don't care, but you're not giving their performance the kind of scrutiny that you'll be giving to the speakers and the host as they share their expertise from the spotlight. From your seat in the audience, you're not likely to remember too much about the emcee as an individual performer because their job is to highlight and enhance the performances of others and keep you engaged with the bigger vision of the event.

The emcee steps into the spotlight over and over again without stealing the show.

SIDE NOTE:

Throughout this book, I refer to myself and others who step into the role as an "emcee"—using the spelled-out version of the acronym, "MC." MC and emcee can be used interchangeably. It's my personal preference to identify myself with the word over the acronym. If you happen to feel different and refer to me as an MC instead of an emcee, it's okay. I'll forgive you, just like I forgive everyone who puts an "h" at the end of my name, which is only a big deal if you're typing my email address.

People Focus

When I attend events, I'm not always there with intentions to meet everyone in the room. Most of the time, when I attend an event, I'm there to meet the right person at the right time for me. It's important to focus on the people aspect of your event because without people, what are we even doing here?

A local group of entrepreneurs in my community spent a couple of years producing quarterly one-day events that drew in a large, engaged audience every time. Their intention with their organization called, "Young Guns," was to bring together entrepreneurs of impact to learn and grow together. They offered a morning general admission event followed by a VIP lunch for an upcharge. What I realized after the first event, where I didn't upgrade my ticket, was that the lunch portion of the event was *not* about the food.

Someone at that event shared with me that their intention to attend the VIP lunch was really about having access to the VIPs like the speakers and event hosts. It was also about building relationships with the other people who saw and treated themselves as VIPs. The person who shared this valuable insight with me was ready to level up and knew that in order to become a VIP herself, she needed to be surrounded by the folks who were doing the things that she wanted to be doing, the people who were willing to go further than the average attendee in the main room.

Every Young Guns event that followed found me attending the VIP lunch and any additional afternoon sessions they added as they grew. To this day, if I am at all able to upgrade my ticket to a VIP experience, I will. And it usually has absolutely nothing to do with the speaker or the content being offered—it's because I want to be in the company of other VIPs. They set an example of what's possible in life and business so that I can find my way to my next level. I've also experienced astounding collaboration opportunities that have come to me as a result of building relationships in these VIP spaces.

The most important thing to remember when building your event is to keep your focus on your people. Even if you're the one in control of the microphone, taking the stage as your own emcee, you must remember that you are *not* the center of the performance. This is one of the top mistakes that I see amateur event hosts make when they decide to take on the job of the emcee. They're hosting the event in order to grow their business so they believe that more stage time equals more credibility and that more of their voice leads to more demand for their products or services. This is not always the case.

When speakers and sponsors have been invited to share the stage at your event, they expect to be showcased equitably. If they spend the whole time feeling like they're playing second fiddle to your tooting horn, they'll leave the experience with a sour taste in their mouths. They won't be as connected to the event, your mission or your brand, and they won't invest with you in the future or recommend your event to others in their network. Sponsors who feel shunned won't return. Attendees who feel like they've been beaten excessively over the head with the hosts message will feel blindsided or taken advantage of, and they may learn little from the other speakers (some of whom you may have paid big bucks to include in your program).

Lead from the stage. Don't steal the show.

6
LEADING FROM THE STAGE

"The most powerful leadership tool you have is your own example."

— John Wooden

WHETHER YOU HIRE A professional emcee, step up to the challenge yourself or nominate one of your colleagues to do it, being an emcee, much like being a great leader, is not about you... and it's all about you.

Commanding the microphone and owning the stage is an act of leadership first and foremost. You are being trusted with a diverse group of people who are coming together from all kinds of backgrounds and circumstances. Each individual is bringing their own biases, baggage and expectations in with them, and your job is to make sure that every single one of them feels like they're part of the action and crucial to the success of your event. You can't do that when all of the focus is on you. How *you* look. What *you* say. How important *you* think *you* are.

On the other hand, you can't step on stage acting like someone else and expect the audience to trust *you* to guide them through the experience. You must be yourself. In fact, you need to be yourself *and more*. When you're leading people from point A to point B, whether it's on a sales call, in a board meeting or at the dinner table, if your audience ends up at point Q, it's your fault.

In his viral TEDx Talk,[1] Peter Anderton shared the two rules of leadership: "It's not about you," and, "It's only about you." Your event is about you for one or more of the reasons we covered in Part 1. And it's about the other people in the room. It's about the other people. And it's about how *you* get them from where they are to where they need to be.

When you're the glue that holds an event together, you're the actor and the stagehand. You're the speaker and the listener. You're the giver and the receiver.

When you're the producer or organizer of a large conference or event, there are many responsibilities that fall onto your shoulders. Most event hosts don't realize how much extra time and effort is required to emcee on top of everything else you're already doing. If you've never considered that emceeing requires its own complete skillset, all of the extra duties will sneak up on you as you learn and lead through the production process.

Black Belt Lesson #872

I've mentioned that my very first emceeing gig was a three-day women's business and empowerment event. Working with the host, I knew that the event was always meant to go beyond surface-level and inspire deep transformation for guests and speakers alike. I knew that my job was to set the tone with an opening welcome, hold space for meaningful insights and spotlight inspirational moments as they hit.

---

1. Anderton Peter, "*Great Leadership Only Comes Down to Two Rules,*" filmed July 25, 2016, TEDx Derby, https://youtu.be/oDsMlmfLjd4

I thought I would be so nervous stepping onto that stage into the role of emcee. It surprised me when I wasn't. I kept waiting for the jitters, the butterflies, the heartbeat in my ears. It never happened. Not once. I stepped onto that stage, welcomed the room, and I had the time of my life!

One reason I was so comfortable on the stage was due to the leadership training I had received in the years prior. I have been involved in martial arts since 2015, when my oldest son started taking youth karate classes as a "Young Achiever." What our family loves about the karate school is their emphasis on communication and leadership skills for even the youngest "Little Ninjas," some of whom were only three years old. The skills that these students learn as preschoolers are skills that I had never explicitly been taught in over 30 years of my own life! In the beginning, I learned a ton just from sitting on the sidelines and observing my children's classes twice a week. After a couple years, I became more involved. I enrolled in adult martial arts classes and eventually joined the instructor training sessions. I attended as many special leadership and communication events as possible. I went all in.

When I first began my instructor training, I was an orange belt. (For reference, in our school, orange is the third belt a student earns out of 13, the 13th belt color being the black belt—the one most people are familiar with and impressed by.) I was new to my own training, and my instructors saw something in me that warranted extending an invitation to me to learn to lead. I said yes because I saw what the leadership and instructor training classes were doing for my son, who had also been invited to learn to lead at his level. I loved it for him. I loved it for me, too.

The reality of stepping into an instructor training class filled with experienced, advanced-degree black-belt instructors was more than a little bit intimidating. I felt so self-conscious when I had to get up in front of the group to say or do *anything*. I did it anyway, though, because I decided that I wasn't going to get on my 7-year old's case to do something that I wasn't willing to do myself.

I felt self-conscious about my performance as an instructor (even though I never taught a single karate class until much later) for several months. I was afraid that all the other instructors were looking at me and silently judging me. I was sure they would find out I was not good enough. I figured that, inevitably, a critical mistake would derail my path to leadership in my own life. I didn't even want to think about teaching an actual kids' martial arts class— especially in front of their parents!

I was so wrong.

No one was judging me. Mistakes were encouraged. I learned to lead my life, and I did end up teaching some kids' martial arts classes.

After a few months of high-level instructor training, I began to realize that I was spending so much time focused on my own performance that the other people in the room were hardly on my radar. I began to understand that in order to be a good leader and an effective instructor, my success had more to do with how the students improved than it did with whether or not I performed perfectly. My purpose as a leader and instructor became bigger than my fear of judgment or failure, and that's when my training truly began.

With Purpose

When I stand at the front of a room with all eyes on me, it's not me they're looking for. They're looking for themselves—for how they can transform their own lives, businesses or perspectives.

Most people are WAY more concerned about themselves than they are about you. And if they do seem to be more concerned about you than about themselves, they're either selling something or hiding something.

When you stand at the front of a room to guide and lead an event, conference, celebration or convention, your primary purpose is not to show the audience who you are. Your role is to show the individuals in the room who *they* are, and in the process, you end up sharing yourself with them, too. Reflect their potential back to them. Show them their capacity for growth, inspiration and impact, and they'll remember you well, too.

I clearly remember the moment I understood the truth of leading this way. It suddenly hit me that all my fear and self-consciousness would never be as big as what the people in front of me needed in order for them to grow. From there, it was a simple matter of unlocking the best way for them to receive the information I had to share.

Confidence comes when your purpose becomes bigger than your fear.

My purpose as an emcee wasn't to put on a great show for my own benefit. Neither is yours. Your purpose as an event host, producer or leader is to take your audience from point "eh" to point "BE," and leave them better than you found them. They're coming in average and hoping to leave exceptional. Your job is to show them what that looks like for each and every one of them, which is no small task.

Are you up for the challenge?

Listen Up

The best leaders are listeners. They take feedback and make adjustments based on what they're hearing, seeing or sensing. As you're leading your event, don't forget to listen. Listen to what people are saying, what they're telling you or your team about why they're in the room. Listen to the good, the bad and the ugly, and adjust accordingly.

The saying that you have two ears and one mouth applies as much to speaking and leadership as it does to the other relationships in your life. When you listen more than you speak and listen to understand, you learn. Really listening to people shows that you care about them. Listening establishes trust, strengthens trust and deepens relationships.

As you move through your event, interacting and engaging with people, make sure to pay attention to what they're saying as well as what they're not saying. If you're hearing more complaints than compliments, investigate. If you're hearing more compliments than complaints, investigate that, too. The truth usually lands somewhere in between.

What I love about being a listener when I'm leading from the stage is that I'm not the only one responsible for creating an awesome event experience. Considering the comments, questions, concerns and challenges of the people I'm sharing the space with helps me to know how to communicate with them more effectively, meet them at their level, speak their language and make sure that I exceed their expectations. I can't know what they expect unless I listen to them!

7

PRESENT YOURSELF

"Don't be afraid to be amazing."

— Andy Offutt Irwin

LET'S TALK ABOUT YOU. When you're the face of your event, you own the spotlight, and at the same time, you're spotlighting other speakers in order to reinforce your reputation as an expert among experts. In Part 1, we talked about why you want to host your event and how you're going to present your expertise in the way that only you can. I hope you gave those questions some thought because this chapter is all about you as the host, emcee and leader.

Let's start with one of the toughest questions in the history of humanity:

Who are you?

How would you describe the value you bring with you when you enter a room? Even if no one remembers your name, how do they feel after interacting with you?

At a conference or event, you want people to feel welcome, excited, interested and comfortable being themselves. This is exactly why you need to make sure that you are being yourself, too. If you've ever struggled with something called "imposter syndrome," which all the coaches and social media gurus seem to be discussing these days, you might question whether being yourself is enough. (Spoiler alert: it is.)

The thing about hosting an event is that you absolutely must bring your most authentic self to the stage. You also need to be more than yourself. You need to show up as your ideal self. The most expansive and aligned version of yourself. If you've never explored this aspect of yourself, you're about to become deeply familiar with feeling like an imposter!

Throughout the planning and preparation process of producing your event, there are hundreds of times when you might consider giving up, canceling the whole thing and never trying anything like it again. You might tell the story that you're not cut out for the spotlight, that you don't have enough connections, that you won't add any new or significant value to the discourse in your area of expertise. These are lies that your mind is telling you to keep you comfortable, safe and small. Don't believe them.

You may argue that showing up to your event as more than yourself is inauthentic. It's not. In his book, Becoming Supernatural, Dr. Joe Dispenza talks about how mental visioning can change the body.[1] Spend some time envisioning yourself at the next level, as the star of the show, as your favorite self. What kind of presence do you want to have on stage? What kind of experience do you want to create for your audience? It's time to become the next version of you. You will show up in an authentic way because the core of you remains the same. You're taking your unique spark and igniting it. You're being yourself and more.

If you're an enthusiastic person, add more enthusiasm or play with different ways to express your enthusiasm. If you are some-

---

1. Dispenza, Joe. *Becoming Supernatural: How Common People Are Doing the Uncommon.* Carlsbad, CA: Hay House, 2017.

one who smiles a lot, smile more, smile bigger, smile with your eyebrows and hands. If you're creative, invite the audience to co-create their experience with you. The bonus of building and hosting your own event is that it's not only the audience who gets to be challenged to grow and expand—you do, too!

3 Keys to Confidence

Imposter syndrome is a thing that has only recently come into the collective awareness. I haven't met anyone yet who has never struggled with feeling like a complete and total fraud. If you're unfamiliar with this phenomenon, "imposter syndrome" is the conscious or unconscious belief that no matter how much you produce or achieve, you're not qualified or worthy of your current position or role, not good enough to get promoted, receive certain accolades or take on more important responsibilities. There's a nagging fear that you'll be "found out" or revealed as an "imposter" somehow, which prevents you from tackling certain projects or pursuing new or exciting opportunities.

I'm certainly no stranger to struggling with imposter syndrome. In fact, as I'm typing this right now, I'm positive that I don't know enough about speaking, performing and emceeing to fill a whole book on the subject, much less write any kind of book that people would actually want to read... and here I am, doing it anyway. What can I say, I practice what I preach!

That's the first step to beating imposter syndrome. Take action. You've already said yes to the responsibility of emceeing and hosting your important event, so let's start with that.

When I was hired for my first gig, I went online and typed something like, "how to emcee," into my search engine of choice. Feel free to do that, too. Ask ChatGPT or your favorite AI companion. You'll get some pretty basic answers that don't necessarily address the mindset and energetic components of the job. You'll have to add your own flavor. Even this book can't do it all for you. It takes a certain level of commitment to step out with confidence and do the job to your highest level possible.

Remember, it's not about you. And it's all about you.

You need to lead from the stage, and you need to start with yourself. Building your confidence is important because people don't trust people who don't trust themselves. Confidence is the outward expression of an internal self-trust.

There are three keys to confidence, and they are pretty simple. I learned them when I heard my sons' karate instructors teach them to the little kids' classes. They're easy to remember and deeper than they seem at first glance.

The three keys to confidence are:

    1. Practice.

    2. Practice.

    3. Practice.

Allow me to elaborate. The more you practice, the better your skills get and the more you can trust yourself not to mess up under pressure.

The first practice is all about learning. If this is the first event you're emceeing, you're going to be nervous. And you're going to screw up. It's not going to be perfect. Practice learning. Get the basics down. Learn where to position the microphone so that you're not too quiet or too loud. Don't walk in front of the speakers while your mic is hot. Follow the script. Watch out for filler words like, "um," "like," "kind of," "you know," "now," "right?" and "so." Practice stage movements and hand gestures. Get a feel for expressing yourself in different spaces. Practice slowing down for gravitas or emphasis and speeding up your pace for energy and excitement. Go down the list that you got from your internet search or AI prompt. Practice learning. Practice the basics. Notice what works. Notice what sucks.

The second practice is about repetition. If you can't repeat what you've learned, have you really learned it? Notice where other speakers hold their microphones. Notice filler words. Get an accountability buddy and speak to each other for varying lengths of time and call each other out when you hear your personal default filler words. Make it fun, get a buzzer or gamify it. Practice what to do with your hands. Practice in front of a mirror. Practice in the park. Practice remembering what the script said without looking at it. Practice people's names. Make sure you're pronouncing them correctly and repeat them, and then repeat them again.

The final practice is about pressure. Add pressure to your practice. Find a way to turn it upside down or do it backwards. Stand on your head. Start at the end. Change the timing. Practice in front of your most judgmental family member or coworker. Practice live on social media. Practice under pressure. That's when you know that you know that you know. When you finally get to the pressure of the real event, you'll be ready for anything.

Confidence is about practice, learning, repetition and pressure. It's also about trusting that you know more than you think you know. Especially if you feel like an imposter sometimes. You do know more than you think you know. You're stronger than you think you are. And the great thing about performing in front of an audience is that the audience generally has no clue how everything is really supposed to go, so even if you mess up, the odds are pretty good that no one will even notice.

One final piece of the confidence puzzle is feedback. If you're not getting direct feedback from another person, it's important to give feedback to yourself. After your practice session or after the event itself, take five minutes to ask yourself two questions and honestly answer them:

What did I like about my performance?

and...

If I had it to do all over again, what would I do differently?

Be real with yourself, and work on that second thing the next time you practice or perform. This is how you grow and build confidence in yourself. Not by dwelling on all the ways you suck at emceeing, but by focusing on what you liked and did well and choosing one thing to change or improve for next time. Each time you practice or perform, use these questions, and you will surprise yourself with how quickly you get to the next level... and the next one and the one after that.

Stage Presence

Owning the stage and making an average event awesome requires attention. Your tone, word choice and body language could be the difference between an enraptured audience and a lost one. I heard some attendees at a recent conference express concern that they felt "yelled at" when the emcee became frustrated by an audience who wouldn't settle down after a break and sharpened his tone of voice. Pay attention to your emotions and keep them under control. The microphone amplifies everything.

As for body language, there's a sweet spot between hyper and monotonous. You need to know what to do with your hands.[2] Don't hide them in your pockets or behind your back. Use enough gestures so that you don't look like a robot, and not so many that you resemble a Muppet. Make eye contact with people if you can see them through the stage lights. Smile when you speak. Dance when there's music. Encourage applause.

When you move around the stage, make it purposeful. Don't wander. Walk to a spot, plant your feet and stay there for a few sentences before moving again. One of the main differences between professional speakers and emcees is the writing and preparation of a formal talk. When you're working on your keynote speech, movement can be practiced and rehearsed. As an emcee, you're mostly ad-libbing, and when speakers are new or nervous, they tend to pace. They tend to meander because standing still can feel vulnerable and scary. However, when you stay present with both feet firmly in place, you appear more confident and authoritative. You are seen as trustworthy and in control.

When I was learning to teach karate, new instructors were always advised to be aware of the "golden birdcage," which is the middle area in the front of a class where they feel most comfortable. They can see everyone, and everyone can see them. Early in their training, instructors spend a lot of time pacing in front of the room in that golden birdcage.

The stage itself can become the golden birdcage in the sense that up front and center or behind a podium is often where the host or emcee feels most comfortable. In my experience, the stage is the best place to be when making important announcements

---

2. "You are Contagious | Vanessa Van Edwards | TEDx London," YouTube video, posted by TEDx Talks, June 27, 2017, https://youtu.be/cef35Fk7YD8.

and introducing speakers. By now, though, I hope you know that emceeing is much more than these two things.

As an emcee, I've spoken from all corners of the room. I run the microphone between tables when the audience needs to speak up, ask questions or share their takeaways. I have found myself sitting on the edge of the stage or interacting with the audience from the floor in front of it. I've pulled out my phone and gone live on social media in the middle of a fundraiser (with the host's permission, of course). I've started talking from the back of the room as I make my way through the crowd. I do what I can to keep myself from getting too comfortable in the golden birdcage, which keeps the audience on their toes and engaged.

The golden birdcage concept applied to events means thinking outside the "box" of the stage. There's a balance to this, like every-thing else. Spend too much time off stage and you could lose some control. Spend all your time stuck to one spot, and you risk becoming a bore. There are many ways to leave the birdcage. One that works exceptionally well while building relationships with the people in the room is to take advantage of the times when you're off stage to sit at different tables or mingle with different people throughout the course of the event. Many events have reserved seats or tables for VIP guests, speakers, staff or volunteers. Just because a table has your name on it doesn't mean you have to sit there. Be a rebel. Those people probably already know you, and you know them. Meeting new people helps you keep a pulse on the energy of the room, gives you ideas for how to navigate transitions, what jokes to tell, how to phrase announcements or how to handle the next hiccup in the agenda. It provides more opportunities to listen.

When you do this early enough in the day, you won't be speaking to a bunch of strangers. You make a large room feel more intimate. Imposter syndrome will try to convince you that the audience is out to get you, that they want to see you fail and judge you for it. When you share offstage moments with individual humans, you learn how much they want to see you shine. You learn what they expect so that you can do your best to deliver it. You learn that all that separates you and them is that you've got a microphone, and they don't.

The Power of Silence

Most people are uncomfortable with silence, especially when they're holding a microphone. It can be tempting to keep talking long after you've finished saying what needs to be said. Is this something you do? Think about it.

Some of the best professional speakers I know are the most adept at incorporating silence.

Silence? Yes. Silence.

Much like powerful leadership leverages listening, impactful speakers leverage silence.

In visual art or graphic design, a visual composition is enriched when negative space—the space between objects—is carefully considered. For example, when I first noticed the arrow in the FedEx logo, it blew my mind. It's a brilliant use of negative space. And if you haven't seen it, look between the "E" and the "x" next time you see one of their trucks on the road.

An emcee's performance requires balance. Balance between leading and following. Balance between sticking to the script and leaving room for magic. Balance between speaking and listening. Balance between sound and silence. When you speak, a poignant pause can punctuate a powerful statement. Slowing down and using silence wisely gives your words gravitas. Especially when an event is packed full of value, content and brilliant speakers, offering a strategic moment or two of silence can help the audience catch up, keep up and get ready for what's next. As with body language, you need to play around a little bit in order to find the sweet spot between emphasis and awkwardness. Trust me, it's a fine line.

Leaving a few seconds of silence after asking a question begins to make the audience uncomfortable, which is exactly where you want them to be so that someone will raise their hand and offer a response. Hold the silence a second or two too long, though, and they begin to move beyond uncomfortable into quiet freak out, which is where you lose them. They might wonder if you've lost your place or forgot what you're trying to say. They could stop trusting you to lead them. It's a very, very fine line, and you will cross it. The good news is that you can always find your way back with some keen self-awareness and by continuing to practice and adapt.

Calm in the Chaos

If you do lose your place or something else crazy happens, don't panic. A lot of the skill required of an emcee involves keeping your composure when things go sideways. Never reveal to the audience that you're struggling. Don't tell them that you're new at this, lost or feeling nervous. That information is on a need-to-know basis, and your audience—who is looking to you for leadership, expertise and guidance—does not need to know. They don't want to participate in your panic—even if they sense it, they want to see you press on and overcome it.

Your audience does not need to know the details of your doubts, fears or current mental state. If you haven't practiced enough to have the confidence you need by the time you get on stage, what have you been doing? If you spill your guts about it to them, they'll know that they weren't enough of a priority for you to put in the prep work, and that is not how you want your VIP guests to feel during or after your event.

Something will inevitably go wrong during your event whether you're on stage or off. When it happens, stay positive and either keep the audience's focus elsewhere or provide as much information as they need to know.

You must never go negative, no matter what's going on around you. If you badmouth a speaker, a sponsor, a coworker, a manager, a vendor or a client, you'll regret it. The only thing you might be able to get away with blaming if you sell it right is technology. Everyone loves to hate technology. Even then, you need to be careful what you say if something weird happens with the tech. You absolutely do not want to ostracize your tech team or appear as though you're blaming them for the issue rather than the quirks of technology in general. Go ahead and make a joke about technology being great when it works—as long as you don't forget to publicly shout out your amazing tech geniuses who are frantically trying to correct the issue in real time.

Have Fun

When you're having fun, your audience will follow suit and have fun, too. Your humor and energy might not be everyone's cup of tea, and it doesn't have to be. The best thing you can do for your event is to go on stage and have a good time. When you're on the mic, put your worries away. The details, logistics and the rest of your responsibilities can wait.

Audiences can tell when you're not all there on stage, so you need to be fully present in order to have a powerful stage presence. Stay in the moment and be with your people. Laugh when things are funny and be the biggest cheerleader in the crowd. Initiate standing ovations because even when you're not on stage and the mic is turned off, the audience is still watching you. Be involved.

It's easier to have fun on stage when you're proud of your prep work and confident in your craft. When you know what to say, how to say it and why you're saying it, you'll have room to breathe and play a little bit. Honor the fact that you will never be speaking to the exact same audience again and treat the experience like the unique expression of connection that it is. Even if the last thing you want to do is emcee this event, you must find something you enjoy about your experience in order for the audience to enjoy theirs.

Learning disguised as play is the most effective kind—even for adults! Help people level up without them realizing they're doing it until after they've done it, and they'll appreciate you all the more for it.

When you're having fun, your pace will naturally ebb and flow. You won't rush through important information, and you won't drone on and on. Vary your pace and pitch to stay in control of the energy of the room. A quicker pace and higher pitch builds energy and excitement while a slower pace and lower tones provides a more calming experience. There are times when how you speak is more important than precisely what you say.

When you're having fun, you give your audience permission to have fun with the deep work they may be doing at your conference or event. Laugh, encourage laughter, and your stage presence will be irresistible.

You, Amplified

So... who are you?

You might think that highlighting speakers, cheerleading sponsors and spotlighting the event's mission means that you have to low-light yourself or shrink into the shadows. This is most certainly not the case. You need to stake your claim to the stage and own your role as the face of your event. Be real, be authentic, be yourself the way you always wanted to be.

Make sure to show up to the rehearsal and get a sense of what the room feels like. Picture it full of your favorite people and make a physical connection with the stage. While it may seem like a simple act, stepping onto the stage, walking through the room and taking a few minutes to embody your amplified self helps you feel like you truly belong. It gives you a fuller sense of ownership over the event and the role of emcee. Your energy and sense of yourself will expand to fit your vision.

Close your eyes. Take a breath. Imagine the applause. Imagine yourself at the end of your event, buzzing with satisfaction and success. Open your eyes. Test the microphone. Test the tech. Meet with your production team. Thank them for making you and everyone else look so damned good.

Dress for Success

One of the most common questions that speakers and emcees ask is, "What do I wear?" To wrap up our discussion of stage presence, let's answer it.

Figuring out what to wear can be one of the most stressful parts of preparing for an event. If you've done similar events in the past, you already have an idea about what type of attire is appropriate. Start there and add your own flavor. Every performer has their own personal preferences or a signature style. Quinn Conyers, an amazing emcee, is known for her impressive sneaker game and bright, colorful outfits. Certain occasions call for bold pops of color and others call for a more muted palette. Regardless of the event, here are few general tips to keep in mind when picking your outfit:

- If you'll be wearing a microphone (lavalier or headset), make sure you have a belt or waistband on which to clip the battery pack. If you're a woman, failing to take the microphone into consideration could get awkward if you choose to wear an unbelted dress.

- Avoid overly complicated attire. Deep plunging necklines, complex patterns or many layers might not be great for photos/video or for sending a message of professionalism and composure.

- Don't wear a lot of jewelry. Large earrings can interfere with headset microphones and necklaces can bump against lavalier or lapel mics. Keep it simple. Find clothing that looks polished enough without a lot of additional accessories.

- Dress up a little bit more than the guests at the event without stealing the entire spotlight. Your wardrobe should be similar to what the speakers are wearing and different enough that you still stand out.

- The most important thing to do is wear something that makes you feel comfortable and confident. Whatever you wear should make you love looking at yourself in the mirror.

Part 3

RUN THE SHOW LIKE A PRO

8

COME TOGETHER

"The conductor of an orchestra doesn't make a sound. He depends for his power on his ability to make other people powerful."

— Benjamin Zander

W E'VE ALREADY DONE SOME work around your event's goals, vision and theme. We've defined what a successful event looks and feels like for you. You might be focusing on ticket sales, price points, upsells, educational materials, sponsorships and power partners, balancing day-to-day business operations, marketing, management or any number of the other responsibilities necessary for the successful execution of this event. Do not forget to think about the people involved in all those areas and more. If you don't intentionally engage with the people, your event will fall flat, you'll fall short of your goals, and you'll be forgotten in a matter of moments.

People don't care how much you know until they know how much you care. Fail to care about the people supporting you and your event, and they will fail to care about you or your event.

The people actively involved in event production include: the event host or hosting organization, sponsors or success partners, speakers, vendors and guests.

As the emcee, it's my job to be a bridge between all these people. I bring everyone together for a common purpose and get them all on the same page. Each individual will come in with a different connection to the event, and the collaborative role of the emcee is to make sure that each person takes actions that complement the larger vision in order to elevate everyone's experience. As the host coordinates logistics, the emcee greets the crowd with a welcoming smile and an open heart. When you're taking on the role of both, make sure that the management of all the logistics doesn't pull your attention away from serving the people in front of you.

Your connection with the people involved in your event begins long before any of them walk through the door. In all your conversations with your vendors, speakers, sponsors and potential or confirmed guests, try to learn at least a little bit about where they're coming from and what brought them into your world. Ideally, each speaker, sponsor and guest is excited to be working with you or attending your event. The conversations you have with them should enlighten you and inform your program.

When I'm emceeing an event, I always plan to show up early and attend any VIP experiences or bonus sessions to engage as many people as possible in conversation. This improves my own performance, and it makes them feel important, seen, heard and understood. It shows them that their experiences are important to the host or hosting organization.

A great question to ask when mingling with people offstage is, "What brought you here today?" Ask. Listen. Remember their answers. Talk about it from the stage when appropriate. Let's dive a little bit deeper into how to cultivate positive relationships with the people you'll be interacting with throughout each phase of your event.

Sponsors

Most events don't run without their sponsors. I've seen some events refer to their sponsors as "success partners," and no matter what you call them, they're your bread and butter. You want to find sponsors who win as a result of collaborating with you so they'll stick with you for the long haul.

Sponsors invest in events for many reasons. If I'm sponsoring an event, I need to know what kind of bang I'm getting for my buck. Who is in the audience? How will I interact with them? How much pre- and post-event exposure do I get? Can I offer my product/service and within what boundaries? Can I have a vendor table or booth? Am I expected to speak on stage and for how long? How many of my ideal clients are in the room?

Your sponsorship packages should address all of these questions. For some sponsors, time on stage is the most important thing. For others, it's the marketing and media exposure before and after the event. Some might not care how they're acknowledged—they just want to be part of this thing you're creating because it's so amazing! You need to find out which of your sponsors are which.

Every one of your sponsors is important, no matter their level of investment. When showing your appreciation for your sponsors, do it with genuine gratitude and respect. Pronounce the individual or company names correctly and confirm that you have an accurate description of their product, service or story. Your sponsors expect to benefit in some way from their investment in your event, and sales don't happen when people don't come first. Work with sponsors who align with your values, gather people together who are likely to want and need their products and services, and your partnership becomes a win-win scenario.

Most consumers are sick of feeling sold to. This doesn't necessarily mean that they don't also want to buy from you or from your sponsors. In fact, I'm much more willing to buy from someone I've met in person than from a faceless company online with a similar product or service. When it comes to larger companies or those with luxury level products or services, look for sponsors who are willing to show up in person at your event, and your attendees will thank you for the opportunity to connect with them. If you're pursuing large national brands as sponsors, it doesn't hurt to ask if they have a local representative who may be willing to attend.

With artificial intelligence becoming more and more prevalent, we humans are waking up to how important it is to have real-life person-to-person interactions. It's become harder to form relationships online because we can't always trust that there's another human being on the other side of our screens. Big brands can give your event a huge boost of credibility and legitimacy, but don't underestimate the value of smaller, local sponsors and partnerships. The best events tend to attract a mix of both.

5 TIPS TO SATISFY SPONSORS

1. Say their names. Find any excuse to thank them out loud into the microphone from the front, back and middle of the room.

2. Share their stories. Talk about why you've chosen to partner with each other and what you admire about the work that they do.

3. Encourage interaction. Invite your guests to connect with the sponsors at their tables or vendor booths, use their promotional codes, take their quizzes or visit their websites.

4. Offer special promotions. Brainstorm ways for your sponsors to offer extra bonus value for your guests in the form of discount codes, limited time offers or swag items that won't end up in the trash.

5. Follow up after the event. Ask how you can make the next collaboration between you and your sponsors even better!

Vendors

You need to hire several people to help you seamlessly execute your event. Even though you're paying them, there's no reason not to treat them as well as your other VIPs.

Your vendors may include venue coordinators, caterers, servers, bartenders, photographers, videographers, DJ/sound production team, printers, florists, event planners, marketers, copywriters, web designers, executive or virtual assistants and anyone else from whom you'll buy a product or service that makes your event special.

It's important to show your vendors respect and treat them as highly valued members of your team. Even if they wouldn't normally attend your event, they could know people who would be a perfect addition to your guest list, so make sure that they have a great experience working with you!

If this sounds like common sense, you probably haven't worked in the service industry lately. News flash—people can be rude. Some people act entitled and make life difficult for those they consider "less than" just because they can. Remember that your vendors are people, too, and you can make or break your reputation in the event space by how you treat them. Vendors talk.

If you're the kind of person who fails to communicate, communicates with an attitude or can't seem to follow basic instructions, you may run into trouble executing your event. For example, you don't want to aggravate the people in charge of your food. We all know why.

If you have had any success in business to this point, you understand that how you relate to people, including each and every one of your vendors, has been a key factor in that success. If you're kissing a sponsor's ass and ignoring the messages from your production team, don't be surprised if you have some "tech trouble" at crucial moments in your program. If you like having a working microphone, make sure you're playing nice with your sound person.

Most event guests pay little attention to the support staff. It doesn't matter. They're still doing essential work to make you look good, so you must pay them attention.

Speakers

There are three types of speakers, and no matter which ones grace your stage, you need to make sure that they are well supported. The first type of speaker is the professional speaker, who gets paid to share their brilliance on your stage. The second is the professional speaker or speaker-sponsor, who will pay you for the chance to talk to your audience. The third is a volunteer speaker, professional or amateur, who offers inspiration or an experience that your audience will enjoy.

Like vendors, speakers talk to other speakers. If they feel disappointed by any aspect of their involvement with your event, whether it's a lack of communication, lackluster promotional efforts or poor production value, they're going to let their speaker friends know about it. Professional speakers expect a certain level of professionalism from you. If your speaker application is confusing or your selection process is unclear, your event may not attract the caliber of speakers you envision.

Each speaker steps onto your stage for their own reasons and brings certain expectations with them. Most professional speakers want to inspire and educate their audiences to help them achieve or overcome something in their lives or businesses. Your speakers want to do well. They want to inspire your audience. They want to be invited back and be referred to other event hosts you may know.

Take care of your speakers.

Take selfies with speakers. Explicitly instruct your photographer to get several shots of them on stage and share those photos with them freely. Communicate early, often and clearly. Let your speakers know how excited you are to see them in action. Offer them snacks. Create opportunities for your attendees to connect with your speakers before, during and after the event. Solicit and provide feedback.

Don't assume that your speakers know everything about what you expect of them, either. Some need to hear instructions and see the agenda more than once. Over-communication is better than under- communication. Set clear boundaries. Make sure they know how much time they have and whether that time includes Q&A. I've seen events go long and audiences get restless because the speaker didn't know or care about the time. Make sure that everyone is on the same page, and your event will stay on time and on mission for the duration! This is a crucial part of the emcee's role.

Audience

Everyone who buys a ticket is a VIP and deserves to be treated like one. Whether you have special VIP tickets or not, each person in your audience has chosen to invest their time and money to attend your event. That's no small thing. Appreciate them for it.

Each guest comes in with their own personal or professional story about why they need to be there. Honor them. Get to know them before and during the event so that you can give them both what they expect and what they really need. As the host, it's your job to know where the group is coming from, some things that they have in common and where you want them to go. Meeting each individual where they are, as much as possible, transforms your event from an impersonal learning session to an experience that sticks with them long after they leave.

Knowing your audience sounds like such a simple thing. When you're facilitating a small workshop for five to ten individuals, it certainly can be simple to check in with everyone directly. When you're hosting an event for hundreds, however, knowing your audience requires more bandwidth. For larger events, offering interactive elements like polls and surveys, smaller breakout sessions or dedicated networking opportunities can help individuals connect with each other as well as with you. We'll talk in more detail about specific engagement strategies in chapter 11.

Your emcee, if you have one, can also do some heavy lifting here. When I'm working in a large crowd, I might not get to talk with every single person, though you'll definitely see me trying! I talk to enough people to get a sense of who they are, why they're there and what they're hoping to see, do or learn. With this information, I help the host deliver what the audience is looking for and more.

It feels more personal, less cookie-cutter, and your guests walk away feeling like the event was custom tailored just for them.

Audiences vary. Some are silly. Some are serious. Some are harder to read than others. Some don't want to engage and others can't get enough interaction. My favorite audiences are the ones who are there to make new connections, broaden their awareness of a topic or experience new levels of growth and expansion.

When people are in alignment and aware of their importance, the room comes alive. People are the heart of the event equation. No matter what they came for, make sure that real, authentic connection is what they get. As technology continues to advance at breakneck speed, it becomes harder and harder to discern what's coming from a real human, especially online. Sharing space with people helps them know who you really are and vice versa.

When you treat your audience right, you create meaningful human connections and memories that last a lifetime, turning strangers into lifelong friends and diehard fans.

9

THE ART AND SCIENCE OF READING A ROOM

"The single biggest problem in communication is the illusion that it has taken place."

— George Bernard Shaw

I F YOU HAVE A conversation with me about running events, you'll usually hear me drop one of my many clever catch phrases, "Anyone can read a script. It takes a professional to read the room." If a person has the ability to read, they can step up to a microphone and read your script. They can read speaker introductions, make announcements and communicate important information. Many emcees read scripts exceptionally well. Newscasters are phenomenal at this, and often when hosts are considering bringing on an emcee, their local news station is the first place they look. News people are trained to read scripts into a camera, though, so not all of them have developed the skill of reading rooms.

Also? Your event is NOT the news.[1]

---

1. https://saradeacon.com/stage-directions/not-the-news

What's the difference between reading a script and reading a room? You probably have a sense of what I mean already, but let's dive in a little bit deeper.

When it comes to your audience, you are positioning yourself as their leader. It's your job to interpret energy, match it and move people where they need to go. You're responsible for the mental, emotional and physical experience of your event. You need to manage expectations and train a random group of people to become the kind of audience that you want. Experts in event experiences can craft great scripts that will deliver 90% without much extra thought or effort on the part of the emcee. However, even the best scripts alone can't bridge that last 10% because they can never accurately predict the thoughts and emotions of the actual humans in front of you. That's why the best room readers are both artfully aware of the human elements and have a working knowledge of the science behind effective communication.

Here's a quick and dirty breakdown to get you started.

Science: The importance of nonverbal communication

As we've already discussed when it comes to your own performance, the majority of our communication is nonverbal. That means things like vocal tone and body language are crucial to your own performance as well as massive clues to help you read your audience. Most people have plenty of bandwidth to read nonverbal cues when having intimate one-on-one or small group conversations. When it comes to bigger rooms, however, you'll have to expand your capacity and watch for certain patterns.

Here are a few examples:

EYES

In a large room, look for people's eyes. When your guests are paying attention, in general, their eyes will be on the stage. You may have a handful of people checking phones or looking down at their notebooks to take notes, which is to be expected. Overall, you want to see more eyes on the stage or speaker than not. When you notice that more than half of your audience's eyes have wandered off to the exit doors, phones or snack table in the back, it's a good indication that you're losing them and it's time to make a shift.

POSTURE

An engaged group of people will be sitting upright or leaning slightly forward while maintaining eye contact or actively taking notes. A disengaged audience may be slouching or shifting in their seats. Maybe they've crossed their arms over their chests, they're checking their phones, getting up to grab coffee or leaving to use the restroom. You may notice people getting antsy close to break times or when a speaker has taken more than their allotted time (or isn't very engaging or coherent with their talk or presentation). Whether you're on stage or off, take note of these changes in posture and adjust accordingly.

MICRO EXPRESSIONS

Have you ever been going about your day pretending like everything was fine when it really wasn't and then had some observant person have the nerve to ask you what's wrong? People might tell you that you wear your heart on your sleeve. Or maybe you've been unable to hide your real opinion because your face said something out loud before you could keep it in check. Micro expressions are small, rapid and often involuntary responses to emotions. If you can see them, they're excellent tools for checking the pulse of your audience. Emotional contagion research has shown that both positive and negative emotions can be passed from person to person as they interact.

At your event, you want to see things like upturned mouths (smiles), nodding heads, open eyes and raised eyebrows. When you start to notice downturned mouths (frowns), furrowed eyebrows, avoidant eye contact, cocked heads or quick glances to others, it's an indication that something about your program is confusing, boring or frustrating.

Art: Verbal response

When you notice any of these nonverbal cues that your audience is not fully engaging with you or the speaker, when you're on the microphone, it's your job to change direction, shift your energy, stop and clarify something or pivot and pick up the pace. If you're in the audience noticing these signals of disengagement, there's not a lot you can do until you return to the stage. What you can do is start to think about what it will take to bring them back and prepare to implement one or more of those ideas once you're back on the microphone again. Set the example and continue to be the best audience member ever, especially when you notice the rest of the room getting restless.

Science: Balancing sound and silence

The average noise level of a crowded conference room or office is somewhere between 70 and 90 decibels. The average human voice is around 60. The library is around 30 decibels. When you're speaking in front of an engaged audience, your voice should be the loudest, ideally amplified with a microphone, and the room should be nice and quiet—not quite library-level, but close.

When the noise level in the room begins to rise, this is another sign you could be losing control of the crowd. It might start with a few polite whispers here and there, hopefully related to the content being presented. Gradually, you'll notice a ripple of sound and movement throughout the entire room. When people start turning to one another and having side conversations, it usually means they're ready for a break or some other physical or mental reset.

Art: Telling people to shut up without hurting their feelings

I hate to admit how many times I've seen an emcee come up to the stage to quiet an unruly crowd and shush them as though they were preschoolers. I hate even more to say that shushing grown professionals like preschoolers can and does sometimes actually work. There are many ways to reset an audience, so consider your approach carefully. When I'm at a conference surrounded by high level professionals and entrepreneurs, the last thing I want to feel like is a toddler who needs to ask permission to address my own basic needs. Two simple ways to grab attention when you need to silence the noise are to increase your own volume or draw out the length of the vowel sound in a single syllable. Either of these approaches provides enough of a pattern interruption to refocus their attention on you without having to resort to, "1-2-3 eyes-on-me" tactics.

Science: An audience in motion

People retain the most information in small chunks. Students attending classes that meet three times a week for 50 minutes learn more than those taking a three-hour class once a week. TED Talks are limited to 18 minutes to optimize the reception of their "ideas worth sharing."[2] WHEN Stories™ are kept under 20 minutes for the same reason: maximum impact in easily digestible chunks of time.

Most conferences include a mixture of longer keynote presentations and shorter breakout sessions. Even during longer keynote presentations, it's usually a good idea to break up the time slot by encouraging interaction and engagement approximately every 20 minutes.

When your audience gets bored, confused or otherwise disengaged, you may notice some bodies shifting in their seats. People will cross or uncross their legs. They fidget with their pens and pencils. They fold and unfold their papers or napkins. Some will get up and walk brazenly around the room to stretch their legs. They might stand in the back for a while or leave altogether to use the bathroom or talk on the phone. Some might lean toward one another to have more whispered side conversations, adding to the noise levels in the room.

Of course no audience is completely still and enraptured for an entire presentation or event, so pay attention when movement begins to take over. That's your cue to shift.

Art: Keeping butts in seats

You definitely want to catch the rustle of movement in a room early so that you can keep the attention and focus where it belongs. Excessive movement will cause even the most focused people in your audience to be mildly distracted at best and to completely disregard your program at worst.

---

2. Carmine Gallo, "Why Your Next Pitch Should Follow TED's 18-Minute Rule," Inc., March 20, 2018, https://www.inc.com/carmine-gallo/why-your-next-pitch-should-follow-teds-18-minute-rule.html.

When you find yourself unable to ignore the audience's fidgeting movements, ideally there is a break coming up. If there's not, find a way to recapture their attention. Ask a random question. Give a pop quiz about the last speaker. Ask if they have any questions. Sing a song. Play some music. Play a game. Every room is different, and your job is to know the room well enough to employ an engagement strategy that works for them.

Level Up Your Skills

Each room has its own personality, its own baseline energy. As an empath, I'm naturally attuned to the energy of the people around me, whether it's one person face-to-face or a room of a thousand. If you're not like me, you may find it more difficult to tune into the energy of a room. It's not impossible. You can develop the skill if you are willing to learn and practice. Even the most oblivious of hosts can get there.

Awareness is key. Notice the shifts in micro expressions, body language, noise and movement. The science sections above are intended to help you pinpoint some of the data around why you might feel something is "off" with the flow of an event or the engagement of an audience. As you find yourself in more and more rooms, whether you're leading from the stage or enjoying an audience experience, your awareness will expand to the point that eventually you won't have to think so much about precisely what you're noticing. From there, you'll develop the ability to anticipate the shifts before they happen. It's not so much about being intuitive or empathetic as it is about building the habit of keen observation.

Courage follows awareness. Reading the room is one thing. Responding and directing a room is the next level. Most people are too nice. They don't want to seem too aggressive or obnoxious. They want to be liked. They want to be nice.

Your audience isn't showing up for nice.

They're not showing up to be coddled and stay comfortable. They're at your event because they know it will challenge them, change them and help them be different. They want to make a difference and leave as better people than they were when they came in. It's not kind to be nice to them. They need you to lead them and guide them and confront them. They want to see how else things can be, and it's your job to show them.

Have the courage to be kind. Call them out. Name the bullshit. If the room is too cold, acknowledge that the room is cold and remind them to grab a sweater at the next break. If the energy in the room is shifting, acknowledge the shift, name what you notice and if it's appropriate, let them know why you're doing what you're doing to bring their focus back.

Most people don't have the courage to name what they notice. The truth is that you're not the only one noticing, and if you ignore what everyone else in the room is aware of, even if it's not conscious on their part, you'll lose their trust. You're all in this together, so stay with them and make sure you're really in it together.

Before I was a speaker and an emcee, whenever I would attend an event, I would choose a seat wondering if it was the "right" one. Most of the time, people plant themselves in one spot at the start, and they never move or stray from it. I never noticed anyone else switching seats, even after they may have realized that it wasn't the "right" spot for them. One time, I set my stuff on an empty table near the front of the room close to the stage. One other person joined me. I was at that event to network and meet people, but I was very new to the scene and lacked the courage to risk looking silly and join a different table. I didn't want the one other person at my table to think I didn't like them, and I didn't want to interrupt another table's established rapport, so I stayed where I started.

I created a story in my mind that this kind of thing might not be something that only happens to me. So when I'm on stage as an emcee, I make a point to notice people sitting alone or the mostly empty tables. I name it when I notice it, and I make sure to explicitly direct people to mingle when I know that they are in the room to mingle. I may even encourage them to pick up their things and switch tables during breaks and mealtimes. While a strategy like that can backfire, overall, it has been a simple way to encourage people to step out of their bubbles and get more out of their event experience.

Name what you notice with courage and confidence.

Keep doing this, and you will show up consistently for and with your audience. People want to engage with you when you practice noticing. Practice naming what you notice. People relate to you because you're challenging them for the purpose of their own growth. Have the integrity to keep showing up as your beautiful imperfect self, doing your best to have fun, engage and relate. Keep noticing. Keep practicing courage in service to your audience, and you'll level up both your emceeing skills as well as develop an impeccable reputation among your peers.

10
SHOWTIME

"The audience doesn't come to see you, they come to see themselves."

— Julianne Moore

B Y THIS POINT, I hope you realize that there's so much more to emceeing an event than speaker introductions, logistical announcements and sponsor recognition. You need to know about these more common aspects of emceeing, too, of course, so let's dive in.

When it comes to event execution, it's still all about the people. During the introductions, announcements and transitions, the main focus is to connect the people in the room with your event's mission, vision and ideal outcome. Without the people's partic- ipation, you're not going to achieve your goals for your event, whether it's raising funds for a worthy organization or creating a space for deep learning and powerful professional or personal growth. What that looks like has as much to do with how you prepare before the event as how you conduct yourself during it.

Leading up to any event, I always make a point to learn as much as possible about the event itself—especially if it's a recurring or annual thing—as well as about the host or hosting organization. I familiarize myself with their themes and goals, and I research (aka cyber stalk) the speakers and sponsors. At a minimum, I'll make sure to familiarize myself with the event scripts and introductions well in advance of my arrival to rehearsal.

I also make sure that any transitions or activities I've been entrusted to facilitate will fit with the mood and theme of the event. I prepare a handful of topics, engagement activities and "break glass in case of emergency" plans so that when things don't go entirely according to plan, I'm able to stay calm and in control.

It's time to talk about the four primary duties of an emcee: introductions, transitions, timing and handling the unexpected.

Speaker Introductions

The main reason most hosts enlist the support of a professional emcee is to introduce their speakers and make announcements. Your speakers will supply you with a current bio and introduction, and at the most basic level, you or your emcee will read it verbatim right before the speaker takes the stage.

When you're emceeing your own event, make sure that you know how to pronounce everyone's names. Every speaker. Every sponsor. Every name. Every company. Every title. Most of the people in the room won't notice or care if you mess it up... unless it's their own name, company name, title or introduction. People are notoriously fixated on themselves 99% of the time, and I truly cannot emphasize this enough.

Say. Their. Names. Properly.

This is how you show them how important they are to you and to your event. It always makes me cringe when someone introduces a speaker and then the speaker gets on stage and introduces themselves differently.

SIDE NOTE:

If you do mess up and mispronounce someone's name or share the wrong information from stage, take full responsibility for your error, and do whatever it takes to make sure it does not happen again.

As much as I'd love to tell you that I've never messed up someone's name, I totally have. A sponsor corrected me during a break, I apologized profusely, and I made sure to shout them out correctly the next time.

If you need to make a public apology or a correction from stage to make things right, do it. Don't hesitate. Set your ego aside and move on. You are human. You're not perfect. Most people won't care, and the one who does care will appreciate your efforts to take ownership and set the record straight.

For many of the events I work with, I go out of my way to get to know everyone who will be speaking. It's sometimes as simple as a quick cyber-stalk, and if I have access to their contact information, I'll request a simple, 15-minute conversation over Zoom. In that short period of time, I'll say something like, "Hi [NAME]—*am I pronouncing that correctly*? Thanks for meeting with me. This helps me get a feel for who you are and the value you'll be bringing to the event so I can hype you up the way you deserve!"

I'll ask three important questions during the course of our conversation:

1. What do you do and how did you get to where you are now?

2. What is the topic of your keynote/breakout/workshop at [EVENT]?

3. What is one thing that you want the audience to know by the end of your session?

I'll also double check if there's anything specific that they want me to emphasize in their introduction or anything that they want me to avoid mentioning at all costs. I'll close the conversation by asking them if they have any questions for me, thank them for their time and let them know how excited I am to meet them at the event.

As the host, you may already know a lot about the speakers you have selected. Perhaps you already have established relationships with them but haven't asked these particular questions. Setting aside time to have conversations like this helps you write your introduction scripts and prepare your general remarks for transitions between speakers. It also shows the speaker that you're taking them seriously, that you see them as an important contributor and that you can be trusted to lead the event with professionalism and purpose. Staying in control of these conversations provides an example of how you are able to stay in control at the helm of the event, too.

Transitions

Most events include a full roster of speakers and a wide variety of activities. As the emcee, your job is to ensure that the transitions between each item on the agenda are as seamless as possible. If the event includes activities in different spaces, make sure you know what's happening, when and where. When you're planning the order of activities, be mindful about the pacing of different parts of the day. Allow for some downtime. Pair deeper learning and heavier topics with something light to release pressure and provide "brain breaks" before diving back into more intense learning. Track the ebb and flow of the energy of the speakers and how they affect the crowd.

Transitioning between deeper, heavier sessions into something more light and fun can be tricky. Honor the weight and depth of those moments without leaving your audience feeling overwhelmed by too much intense emotion or complex information for too long. If they get stuck there, you'll lose momentum, and if you move them out too quickly, you risk appearing superficial.

Putting the theme of your event front and center, as we covered in Part 1, makes this part of your job that much easier. If you have many different types of speakers or a wide range of topics to cover, it will be more difficult to weave everything together and return to the larger theme during transitions. Connecting speakers and topics should happen during the planning of the agenda so that your audience is consistently being reminded about the part they're playing in the bigger purpose of your event.

I once emceed a women's conference with the theme, "Collaborate." The intention behind the entire event was about business, professional and personal growth in relation to others. Everyone in the room was encouraged to explore opportunities through authentic connection, deepening relationships and generously supporting one another.

The theme of collaboration was present in every session from the VIP speaker to the closing keynotes. During transitions between speakers and activities, I reinforced an idea or intention from the previous session that emphasized the importance and relevance of the "collaborate" theme. For example, during speed networking, I directed the attendees to answer specific questions that encouraged the participants to get to know each other on both a personal and professional level. This allowed them to identify things in common that they wouldn't have known otherwise, opened them up to new ways of relating with each other and encouraged them to explore areas of collaboration.

Even if your event takes similar form and shape year after year, you can still layer new themes on top of it. Sometimes, an outside perspective can help you see the common thread woven into your event—even if it's unintentional or unofficial. Strategic selection of your speakers and discussion topics helps you to highlight the patterns and connections between them during your transitions.

As the event unfolds, be aware of how the keynotes, breakouts and other activities fit together and whether your thoughtful planning is paying off or missing the mark. You need to have the courage to pivot in the moment if something isn't landing right with your audience and communicate to make sure that any adjustments you make are appropriate and agreeable to your team.

While speaker introductions, sponsor recognition and common announcements tend to be strictly scripted, transitions usually involve more improvisation. Even if you know each session's topic and takeaways, what the speaker or facilitator presents could be much different than the description they originally provided, so you've got to stay on your toes. You set the example of how you want your audience to behave, so you need to pay the most attention.

Trust your instincts that if something from a session stands out to you, it's something that the audience will appreciate hearing again. If it helps you, take notes during their presentations so that you can share those "aha moments" and emphasize the brilliance and inspiration of the speaker again after they leave the stage.

Effective transitions help an audience lock in and learn. It's often where the magic happens, and magic doesn't always show up according to plan. Follow your intuition. Follow the room's energy. Trust your instincts and take action with confidence.

Prepare well and leave yourself flexible to move where the moment takes you. As an emcee, it's more about familiarization than memorization. Be familiar enough with the content, the agenda, the script and the speaker flow and flexible enough to make changes when necessary. Know your audience. Know your speakers. Know your sponsors. Know your role. Keep the mission in mind so that you can make on-the-spot decisions about the direction of the event that seem effortless. I often thoughtfully consider several different options for transitional commentary or activities that could fit in and keep them in my back pocket (sometimes literally) so that I can pull out the right one at the right moment without skipping a beat.

Preparation is pivotal.

Flexibility is fundamental.

Timing

I attended a three-day conference that was packed full of phenomenal speakers, impactful breakout sessions and super fun bonus activities. The opening address on the first night was scheduled to begin at 6:00pm. The doors to the main conference room were still closed at 6:00. On the second morning, the first session was scheduled to start at 9:00am. People were sitting at their tables at 9:00 and the speaker was not introduced for another 20 minutes.

What do you think happened on the third day of the event?

The main conference room remained conspicuously empty until about 20 minutes after the program was scheduled to kick off.

Why? Because for the previous two days, the hosts had trained us to expect a late start.

Leading from the stage means managing your audience's expectations. When you publish your agenda to the public, your attendees are going to be referring to that schedule throughout your conference or event. If you don't stick to the schedule, your guests will unconsciously learn not to trust you, which could lead to hesitation about working with you outside of the event, too.

Keeping the event on time is one of the most crucial tasks that no one notices when executed flawlessly, and it's the one you'll hear most about on your feedback forms when it's not.

I don't normally wear a watch unless I'm emceeing an event. Whether you wear a watch, have a clock in view or slyly check your phone throughout your event, you need to keep track of the time. Personally, I don't keep my phone on me when I'm on stage because it can be a distraction even from a hidden pocket. There's no guarantee that there will be a visible clock in any given location, either, so I wear a watch. I have one that's very easy to read, even in the dark.

When programs start late or go long, you're unintentionally communicating that you don't respect people's time. It's not only the audience's time, either. If one speaker takes more than their allotted time, that usually means another speaker's spot gets cut short. Don't do that to your speakers.

If you've done your job, prepared well and communicated with everyone involved in your production in advance—at the very least by the rehearsal—they should know exactly how long they have on stage and what happens if they step out of bounds. There are many ways to signal a speaker to conclude their talk, and you get to choose what works for you. However you do it, let the speakers know in advance which signals to watch for. Some events have a monitor that can be seen from the stage with a countdown timer. Many events don't. Use hand signals. Appear ominously at the side of the stage making uncomfortable eye contact with the speaker. Cue the music. Invest in one of those giant hooks to pull the performer offstage by force. Anything can work. Use your imagination.

High level speakers usually get the hint when they see you stand up from your seat, move to the side of the stage or circle a finger in the air in the universal sign for "wrap it up." Inexperienced speakers or those with an air of egoic entitlement might need a more obvious cue.

Carry a copy of the event agenda with you at all times. If you've got your phone on you, keep the file or a screenshot pulled up. I often use both my phone and physical notecards because I don't like to rely solely on technology. You're in charge of timing, so you need to know what's coming next. If someone else tells you to do something that's not on the agenda, make sure that person is a reliable source with the authority to communicate the change before you act on it. If you're confused, the audience will be confused. And in the wise words of every marketing expert ever, "confused minds don't buy." They won't buy into your vision. They won't buy your product or service, and they won't open their wallets for your cause no matter how worthy it is.

Clear communication in preparation for your event leads to clear communication with your audience during your event. Track the time and keep the schedule in mind. When speakers go over time (and they will) or when the unexpected occurs (and it will), your job is to get that train back on the rails as efficiently as possible without letting anyone else in the room know it was off.

The Unexpected

Speaking of the unexpected, your job description as an emcee also includes being the face of calm when chaos happens behind the scenes.

Think of a duck gliding smoothly along a still body of water. There's not much of a ripple on the surface even though their feet are paddling frantically beneath it. You're the duck. You may have to work frantically behind the scenes while giving the appearance of gliding effortlessly through it all.

When things go wrong—and they will go wrong—your audience will look to you for guidance and reassurance.

What do you do when the photographer has a seizure in the middle of a crowded breakout session?

These things can and do happen.

I've been sitting in an audience and felt my "Spidey sense" go off, knowing that there was something amiss even though I couldn't tell precisely what it was. I tend to be very tuned in to the energy of a room, no matter where I'm positioned in it. When I get that feeling that something isn't going according to plan, I watch. I notice. Who is moving with a greater sense of urgency than before? Who is having whispered conversations on the side of the stage or in the back of the room? What are the tech guys doing? How well is the person *on the microphone* addressing the situation or diverting attention from it?

You absolutely cannot plan for every unexpected thing that might happen at any given event. That's why it's unexpected. If you're a type A person, though, I guess you can certainly try to plan for anything. I'm not, so I like to emphasize a general approach to preparation. The difference between preparation and planning in my mind is a matter of rigidity. If you are easily agitated when things don't go precisely as planned, emceeing might not be the best role for you. If something goes wrong and you are deeply affected, it could take you some time to recover. When you're prepared for the unexpected, you can fall back on mindfulness and confidence tools, communication techniques and leadership skills to stay in control even if others panic.

Improvisation is a phenomenal skill for any speaker or leader, whether you're a performer or not. The ability to ad-lib in front of a crowd is a skill that even many professional speakers have not taken the time to master. If you have the opportunity to attend an improv class, I highly recommend you do it. You might feel silly, and you might think that you suck at it. Do it anyway because sucking at something new is always to your benefit.

Do whatever you have to do to feel confident that your experience and skillset will be enough to help you handle at least the most common of unexpected circumstances.

Here's a short list for reference:

- Tech issues—technology is great... when it works

- Speaker issues—delayed arrivals or overtime sessions

- Schedule changes—last-minute additions or cancellations

- Meal service issues—delays, shortages or menu changes

- Emergency situations—alarms go off, a health event

- Logistical issues—missing materials, unclear signage, etc.

- Personality conflicts—parties can't resolve their own issues

- Venue issues—things aren't where they're supposed to be

- Communication issues—stories aren't lining up

- Audience disruptions—big emotions, drunkenness, etc.

- Unexpected VIP needs—travel troubles, bruised egos

- Security issues—outside threats, inside threats, perceived threats

- Weather issues—hurricanes, tornadoes, storms, etc.

- Acts of God—use your imagination

You can never know exactly what will happen during your event or conference. Tech is the one thing that I never completely trust to go 100% smoothly. Therefore, I always have my notes, agenda, introductions and scripts printed out on physical notecards. I carry my cards with me everywhere. I am so stuck to my notecards that at one event, my hands turned pink because I printed my notes on sparkly pink paper to match the brand colors of the event. The paper was a little bit reactive to moisture, I guess!

Aside from tech issues (or sometimes because of them), the number one thing to be prepared to do is to fill time. Some speakers end early. Sometimes the program includes buffer time that turns out to be unnecessary. You can improvise to fill these moments or you can prepare some exercises or engagement activities that align with the event (see the next chapter for some ideas). Give information and direction when it's appropriate, of course, and remember that the idea of the time-fillers is to keep the audience present with you and keep the event flowing as though everything is playing out exactly according to plan.

When it comes to emergencies, look to the venue staff to communicate evacuation procedures. If you've taken first aid or CPR certification courses, rely on your training. Regardless, it's a good idea to have a general awareness of where things like fire extinguishers, fire exits, first aid kits and AEDs are located. This awareness can help you stay calm in the face of crisis situations. When you're in control of the microphone, people look to you and listen to your instructions. Your ability to communicate with authority will help to keep the room calm when things get chaotic. If an emergency arises when you're off stage, people may still look to you to direct them. Do what you can.

Make sure that you know who calls the shots in different types of emergencies. Is it the emcee? The venue staff? Emergency services? Determine your chain of command beforehand whenever possible.

After the emergency has passed, you'll need to determine whether or not to publicly acknowledge what happened and how to acknowledge it appropriately without unnecessary drama. Honor the seriousness of a significant emergency, provide directions for support services when needed and redirect or reset the energy in the room if and when the program resumes.

EMERGENCY TOOLKIT:

Communication is essential in the case of an emergency. Sometimes, people do need to be informed and directed. Preparing a simple emergency communication protocol can help you communicate among staff and volunteers without causing unnecessary panic among guests.

Hand Signals:

- Crossed arms = Security needed

- Touching ear = Audio issue

- Finger across throat = Cut mic/stop immediately

- Tapping wrist = Time's up

- Thumbs up = All clear/ready/proceed

Onsite Texting:

- "Code Red + location" = Medical emergency

- "Code Blue" = Technical failure

- "Code Green" = All clear to proceed

- "Eyes on [person/location]" = Discreet attention needed

Position:

- Designated spots for key support staff/volunteers

- Clear line-of-sight from stage to production booth

- Specific check-in locations to use between segments

Authority Chain:

Clarify in advance who makes the final call in different types of emergencies.

Follow-up:

Decide how to resume the event after an emergency has been addressed, including appropriately acknowledging what happened without dwelling on it, offering discreet support when necessary, etc.

QUICK REFERENCE:

Helpful stock phrases to have on hand when the unexpected occurs.

For Medical Situations:

We are going to take a brief pause. If there is a medical professional in the room, please meet [point person] at [location]. Everyone else, feel free to stretch, check messages or introduce yourself to someone new.

For Technical Issues:

We seem to be experiencing some technical difficulties. While our team works their magic behind the scenes, why don't we [insert activity instruction here].

For Venue Concerns:

I'm probably not the only one who has noticed the temperature of the room. Our team is working on getting that adjusted. In the meantime, feel free to grab a sweater or jacket at our next break which will be in about [number] minutes.

For Unexpected Schedule Changes:

In order to make sure that everyone gets the most value from our program, we'll be moving to [next item] next, and [delayed item] will happen at [new time].

For Returning After an Interruption:

Thank you for your patience and understanding. We're all set to resume our program. Let's welcome [next speaker/next segment].

11

ENCOURAGING AUDIENCE ENGAGEMENT

"Tell me and I forget. Teach me and I remember. Involve me and I learn."

— Benjamin Franklin

HOW DO YOU WANT *people to talk about your event after it's over?*

If you've put in the work to this point, activating your audience should be relatively simple. You know who they are, and you know why they've chosen to attend your event. You've thought about different ways to connect with them throughout your program, and now you need to apply what you've learned so far.

WARNING!

There are a TON of amazing ideas in this book that you could incorporate into your event. PLEASE DO NOT USE ALL OF THEM IN ONE EVENT. When speaker rosters get too long or there are too many different kinds of activities going on, audiences get overwhelmed. They lose sight of the central intention of your event. When in doubt, leave it out!

A simpler event creates opportunities for magical moments like "hallway conversations," where attendees form deeper bonds with each other outside of the main space. A simpler event feels more polished and professional. A simpler event has fewer moving parts, which means fewer chances for things to go wrong. I'll say it again: *When in doubt, leave it out!*

Your VIP Audience

Remember that everyone in your audience is a VIP in their own way, so make sure to highlight them throughout your event. Thank them for being there. Honor their commitment to your cause. Emphasize that they could be choosing to do anything else with their time and you're so grateful that they chose to spend their time at your event. You can also add some special segments in your agenda to further highlight your guests.

- Incorporate contests, raffles or competitions.

- Spotlight individual audience members for achievements related to your theme, contributions or unique perspectives.

- Learn as many of their names as you can and use them. (Don't forget to pronounce them correctly!)

- Shout out your volunteers or anyone else in the room who went above and beyond to show their commitment to your cause.

- Encourage your speakers to include audience participation throughout their talks. They might consider things like live coaching or using some of their time for Q&A.

AUDIENCE ENGAGEMENT DONE RIGHT:

Pat Miller, founder of the Small Business Owners Community, facilitates an "Idea Slam" as part of his signature talk, and it never fails to engage an audience. The "Idea Slam" is a massive group brainstorming session designed to help small business owners solve a business problem right there on the spot. It gets everyone in the room involved and showcases individuals and their businesses with a spirit of encouragement and collaboration. It's so much fun, and all the participants walk away with tangible actions they can implement right away in their businesses!

- Get feedback in real time by inviting the audience to share their stories, thoughts or takeaways as part of your agenda. When I give my "Drama Detox" signature talk, I invite audience members to share their real-life scenarios to illustrate different ways drama shows up and how it can be diffused.

- Set up a giant white board in a prominent place and invite your guests to contribute meaningful or funny quotes throughout the event. Invite everyone to take photos of it and share some of the quotes on social media.

- Highlight unique note-takers. I've attended an event where someone took live "Sketchnotes" during one of the main stage keynotes. At a different event, one of the audience members posted his visual notes online after each speaker. The host shared the posts with the audience during the event to showcase that individual's talent and reinforce the speaker's brilliance.

Whether you're intentionally planning audience engagement activities, or you need some ideas to keep on hand (or in your back pocket) in case the need arises, here's a quick list of some tried and true engagement strategies I've included or experienced at different events:

- Speed networking or table talk prompts

- Sponsor interview or Q&A (if they're open to it)

- Share a relevant article summary, song lyrics or story

- Dance break

- Silly interactive games like 20 Questions, MadLibs, Would You Rather or 2 Truths & A Lie

- Ask the audience quirky or thought-provoking questions

- Let the audience ask you questions

- Simple meditation or visualization exercises

- Chair yoga or other stretching

Use your imagination! Remember, if you're having fun, the audience will be having fun, too—even if you're using these techniques because something's gone wrong behind the scenes. Keep your cool and get playful with it.

Digital Engagement Tools

There is an endless amount of technology available to us that most speakers have yet to leverage for enhanced audience engagement. As I've mentioned, I have a self-proclaimed healthy mistrust of technology in general, as well as some experiences where I couldn't keep myself from being impressed at its capabilities.

When applied strategically and effectively, some of these digital tools can blow everyone's minds and encourage them to connect on a whole new level.

My personal go-to when it comes to digital engagement is offering collaborative photo albums to my clients. I create custom albums for their event, including storage that doesn't require an ongoing subscription or compromise their rights to their own images. When made public, anyone in attendance at the event can contribute photos to these albums. That way, people don't need to be friends on social media in order to see all of the great pictures from the event, they don't need to go searching for hashtags, and the event organizer doesn't need to spend extra time and effort curating and sharing photos in a hundred different places online.

I've seen several speakers incorporate live polling tools to gather relevant, real-time data during their presentations, which personalizes the information for the audience and reinforces the content's impact. Some live polling tools include Mentimeter, Slido and Poll Everywhere, and I'm sure that there are many, many more.

You may want to use games or quizzes as part of your performance to have some fun with your audience and bring out their competitive nature. I've been at team training and VIP events that utilized Kahoot or versions of Jeopardy and Family Feud to share new knowledge or test retention.

QR codes are great for any call-to-action that's included in the program. I'm a huge fan of Talkadot.com for collecting speaker feedback. LinkedIn also has integrated QR codes to facilitate easy connections on the platform during live networking.

Speaking of social media, one of my favorite audience engagement activities is a "Selfie Scavenger Hunt," where each table is provided with a list of poses, places or people to include in their selfies. They're instructed to post on Facebook or Instagram using the unique event hashtag (or encouraged to upload their selfies to the collaborative photo album). Whichever table completes their selfies first gets a prize. This activity merges VIP recognition and digital engagement in a really fun way.

Strategically placed selfie stations with creative backgrounds and props also encourage people to take and share photos of your event, leading to FOMO online and buzz for your next project.

Some events have the budget and talent to create their own event apps. These can include messaging capabilities, interactive schedules and other customized user experiences. A good event app will be useful before and after the event as well as during the experience, so this might not be the way to go if you're on a tight budget or time crunch.

For an extended list of helpful and unique digital engagement tools, visit welcometothestagebook.com/resources.

No matter which engagement strategies you include, the main focus should always be on connection. It can be easy to rely on technology for the illusion of engagement, but if you're not personally present with your people, the distance can cause damage. Check out the tech, narrow it down to a couple of favorites and go with what fits best with your unique event and audience members. Trust your gut, keep it simple and don't forget to have fun! Your audience will appreciate your efforts to include them.

12

ENERGY IS EVERYTHING

"Almost everything will work again if you unplug it for a few minutes, including you."

— Anne Lamott

A CCORDING TO THE AUDIENCE, your event couldn't be going any more smoothly. The speakers are energetic and engaging. The content is fresh and exciting. The tech is novel and impressive. The emotions are ebbing and flowing flawlessly. None of the chaos behind the scenes—the speaker stuck in traffic, the faulty slideshow, the catering snafu—is leaking into your guests' awareness because of how well you've prepared and communicated with your team. You're in control. You're connecting with people. You're anticipating people's needs. You're communicating clearly. You're keeping things moving. You're having fun. You're in the zone. The event is a resounding success!

The next day, you can hardly get out of bed. Your voice is gone. You feel like you've been hit by a truck. You have a short temper with your family and find yourself crying in the grocery store when you can't find any good bananas. Welcome to the crash.

In Part 1, we went through all the different reasons for hosting your event, who it's for, why it matters and what your ideal outcomes look like. In Part 2, We talked about how you need to show up as the host and face of your event and lead with clarity and confidence so that the people in the room connect with you, your vision and each other for lasting impact. We talked about the counterintuitive approach of listening and leveraging silence as a speaker. Here in Part 3, it's been all about the tricks of the trade—putting people first, navigating the practical duties of emceeing your own event and the art and science of reading a room. One last thing you absolutely must attend to is your own energy.

I've held space for a number of intensely emotional and deeply transformational events. Even if nothing unexpected occurs, facilitating such events can be extremely physically, emotionally and energetically demanding.

No matter how adept you are at the technical skills and communication aspects of emceeing, you cannot ignore the importance of preparing, protecting and restoring your own energy. If you've hosted events in the past, you know that they require an enormous amount of energy to pull off. You have probably experienced the "event hangover" or come down with "conference crud" (a cold, flu or other acute illness) after an event is over. The adrenaline disperses, you're left alone with your thoughts and feelings about everything that has happened, and you feel like you could sleep for days.

Most people learn the hard way that you need to build rest and self-care into your event experience.

If you want sustainability in your business, you need to balance energy expenditure with energy restoration—like building muscle requires recovery in between workouts. Hosting requires the intentional management of your energy, from pre-event preparation through the event itself and into the days that follow.

Before the Event

In addition to everything else you're doing to prepare to serve the mission, vision and ultimate goal of your event, you must prepare yourself for the energy marathon of being "on" for the duration of the program.

In the two weeks leading up to an event, I recommend being very intentional with your calendar, your diet and your rest. Decline meeting invitations when they are not directly related to the successful execution of your event or conference. Take the time to eat as clean as possible and drink enough water. Don't neglect your exercise routines any more than absolutely necessary. Go to bed a half hour earlier than usual. Carve out time to meditate or take a few extra naps.

Stress is the number one cause of illness. Do whatever it takes to minimize stress leading up to your event because the last thing you want is for the face of your event to be puffy, coughing and full of snot.

As they plan, a lot of event hosts forget about how much mental bandwidth is required to keep an event running smoothly, even when they're not also the one emceeing. You have a hundred things on your mind, which depletes your mental energy as well as your physical energy.

Sharing the mental load with others helps you sustain your energy reserves. Make sure that more than one person could step in if necessary. Keep a master copy of important information up-to-date and share it with the members of your inner circle or support team. Write things down when you think of them so that you don't rely on your mind alone to remember crucial details. You might think you'll remember that really important thing without writing it down because it's really important. Trust me, you won't.

As someone who is easily influenced by others' raw energy and emotions, I need to make sure that I put boundaries in place before a large event, especially ones that involve a higher level of emotional vulnerability. In order to prepare myself to move through rooms filled with others' energies and emotions, one thing I like to do is visualize myself inside of a bubble. Other people's emotions might touch my bubble, but they can't pass through it. You can download the guided audio of this energy protection visualization exercise at welcometothestagebook.com/resources.

As the emcee of a more emotionally charged event, you need to set your own emotions aside in order to hold space for the audience's emotional experience. Create a meaningful pre-event ritual or visualization that works for you and actually remember to take the time to do it before you walk into the conference room or onto the stage. Your ritual should be short, portable and memorable so that it's easy to repeat wherever and whenever you need it.

During the Event

Events can be an emotional roller coaster. Inspirational and motivational speakers are paid well to take their listeners on a powerful emotional journey. People are often encouraged to self-reflect or share experiences that could be challenging or uncomfortable for them. Many of us are walking into events carrying personal burdens or dealing with circumstances at home or at work that are running in the background of our minds as we move through the event's agenda.

When you're the face of your event, you don't have the luxury to process your emotions in real time. You are the one who needs to keep your composure even if every other person in the room is losing theirs. It's not about denying or avoiding your feelings.

It's more a matter of selective detachment—choosing when, where and how to attend to your own emotional experience.

The day before I went to emcee an important conference, my family experienced a significant traumatic event. I communicated candidly with the event host, I met with my therapist before the start of the event, and I allowed my husband to handle the heavy lifting at home without me. I took the stage as planned, and our guests had no idea what was happening in my life unless I told them directly.

The stage is no place to unpack your baggage.

With that being said, it's important to care for yourself throughout an energetically demanding event. While you need to be "on" for the duration of the event, that doesn't mean neglecting your own basic needs. If you need to step into the hallway to check in with yourself during a video interlude or activity, do it. If you need to do some breathwork during a bathroom break, go for it. If you need to eat lunch outside by yourself so you can collect your thoughts, clear your mind and reset your emotions before the next session, it's okay. Even the busiest events offer micro-moments of downtime you can use to recalibrate your energy.

Simple physical breaks can be the difference between sustaining your energy until the end of an event and finding yourself running on fumes halfway through.

- Step outside for a minute to breathe fresh air and feel the sun on your face.

- Take 5 deep breaths with your eyes closed and both feet planted on the floor.

- Practice EFT tapping.

- Stand in a "power pose" for a few seconds before you step onstage.

- Splash cold water on your face (or your neck if you have makeup on).

- Keep an invigorating essential oil on hand to inhale as needed

- Do a quick stretch like reaching your arms over your head and bending to one side then the other.

Managing your energy throughout an event also means setting boundaries. While you may want to connect with people and be friendly, you don't necessarily need to be everyone's friend. Make sure that your responsibilities are clearly outlined in advance, and if things come up that need to be handled outside of your role and scope, pass the buck to the proper person. You may also encounter difficult or inappropriate situations. Handle them to the best of your ability, try not to take confrontations personally and don't be afraid to call in reinforcements if things get out of hand.

Your energy naturally ebbs and flows a certain way throughout the day. Work with your own rhythms instead of fighting against them, and you'll deliver an energetically aligned experience for yourself and for everyone else in the room.

After the Event

The day after a big event, you might feel like a deflated balloon. There's often a sense of release or relief. Sometimes there's grief that it's over. You might feel proud or disappointed. You might feel elated, inspired, invigorated or drained. You might be itching to implement new ideas or plan the next big event right away. You might never want to think about hosting another event ever again. It's all normal.

I've been guilty of failing to plan for the "event hangover" more times than I can count. When you're clearing your calendar before your event, make sure to clear it for a few days afterward, too. The high of an incredible event is often followed by a crash, which can surprise you if you've never experienced it before.

The day after an event is a good time to give yourself closure. Take some time to journal about what went well and what you would do differently if you had it to do all over again. Send an appreciation text to your team to thank them for all their hard work. Start gathering thoughts and ideas for the next event you plan to do if they come to you. Look through your photo album and post a couple of the best pictures on social media.

Unpack the emotions you set aside during the event. Cry, scream, sing, dance or workout to move those emotions when you feel the urge. Have a cup of tea. Sleep in. Get a massage or spa treatment. Take a nice bath or a long hot shower. Wear your most comfortable clothes. Stay in your pajamas all day. Drink water. Go for a run if that's something you find soothing. Eat something nutrient dense and delicious. Take a nap. Watch something mindless on TV, play a stupid game on your phone or read some light fiction. Take a walk. Of all these suggestions (and whatever else you come up with on your own), choose what works for you and leave the rest. Rest however you rest best.

The days after a big event are not for intense physical, intellectual or professional pursuits.

At the Milwaukee airport, there's a sign at the exit of TSA security that says, "Recombobulation Area." It's our airport's way of ac-knowledging that going through the screening process is disruptive and you might need a moment to put yourself back together. Discombobulation happens during the course of an event, too, and you might need more than a day or two to put yourself back together—mentally, physically, emotionally and energetically.

You'll learn to recognize and support your own energy patterns the more you practice this level of self-awareness. You'll be able to anticipate and communicate your boundaries and limitations, and you'll become more adept at optimizing your energetic patterns for sustainability and success. Events require huge investments of time, money and energy, the latter being a big one that hosts often fail to consider in advance.

Even the most energetically conscious professionals forget to prioritize themselves in certain scenarios, which is why we all need to be reminded about how important it is to share the load. In the next section, we'll explore how partnering with a professional emcee can relieve some of the energetic burden, freeing you to invest your energy even more strategically before, during and after your own events.

Part 4

THE PARTNERSHIP POWER-UP

13

LETTING GO OF CONTROL

"Sometimes letting things go is an act of far greater power than defending or hanging on."

— Eckhart Tolle

N OW THAT YOU'VE LEARNED and extensively practiced everything we've covered so far, you are more than fully equipped to run your own show. Right?

Of course you are highly capable and brilliant, and your next event is going to be beyond incredible because you took the time to absorb all the information in this book.

And... *What if it could be even better?*

Even though you *can* do it all—from planning to production to hosting and emceeing—what if your event could be improved by *not* doing it all?

You already have a ton on your plate. It's time to ask yourself if you're willing to add more. Do you have the time and energy to develop your stage presence and learn to read a room and take an improv class and research technology and create worst case scenario playbooks while controlling the ebb and flow of everyone else's energy too?

You may already be:

- Developing and communicating event objectives

- Creating a budget and keeping costs contained

- Researching, securing, booking and communicating with your venue

- Nailing down dates, times and creating an agenda

- Researching, contacting and hiring speakers and other vendors

- Assembling and coordinating a team of volunteers or staff

- Reviewing and submitting contracts for venues, vendors, sponsors and speakers

- Creating setup and teardown timelines and coordinating execution

- Creating and selling sponsorship packages

- Planning and executing your marketing strategy for selling tickets

- Designing and distributing on-brand marketing graphics

- Managing ticket sales and promotional offers

- Pre-event communication with speakers, vendors, sponsors and guests

- Scheduling post-event follow-up and feedback collection

- Gathering items for giveaways, swag bags or table favors

- Addressing accessibility needs

- Finalizing details like floor plans and stage setup

- Arranging signage and wayfinding

- Preparing for registration, guest assistance and troubleshooting

- Overseeing AV and technical needs

- Communicating with catering and hospitality services

- Engaging with guests and navigating concerns or complaints

- Analyzing engagement and effectiveness of program (post-event)

- Collecting and considering feedback during and after the event

- Confirming all services were delivered as contracted and addressing disputes

- Comparing actual costs to budgeted amounts

- Creating and posting social media or other content to highlight the event's impact

- Sending thank you messages and acknowledgements to volunteers, vendors, sponsors and staff members

- Documenting and organizing materials and processes for future events

- Coordinating the delivery of funds raised to the recipient organization (for fundraisers)

- Leveraging your event to promote your business (for conferences/retreats/business-building events)

Producing a successful event is a big job, which is why a lot of business owners who want to host an event never actually end up doing it. Handling all of the above plus emceeing is totally possible for a badass business owner or nonprofit director like you. You are more than capable of doing all the things. Let's get real for a moment, though. Will you be able to do all the things *well*?

Just because you can do something doesn't always mean that you *should*.

If you absolutely must emcee your own event, start by working your three keys to confidence—practice, practice, practice. Then remember that even if your hands are on all the things, you don't actually have to do all of them by yourself.

Even if you're not ready to hire an emcee, you can still lean on the people around you. If you have volunteers, delegate tasks to them and help them own those tasks. Like many event hosts I've worked with, you might be the kind of person who has trouble letting go of control. We talked about leadership early on, and the best leaders create more leaders. Communicate your vision, your mission and your goals, and let your team contribute their ideas and use their skills to make your event as meaningful to them as it is to you.

For example, your production team has probably worked on hundreds of events, including events similar to yours. Ask them for suggestions, referrals to other vendors or insights about what has worked or not worked at other events like yours that they've seen. Be open. Be curious. I bet they have some great ideas or different perspectives you could use. Whether their suggestions work for you or not, inviting their collaboration will help cultivate a great working relationship with them for now and in the future.

You can learn so much from your vendors about hosting and producing events—about audience engagement and creative ways to collaborate. Your videographer might offer information about content creation, marketing or promotion. Your caterer likely has some wisdom to share about room layout and flow. Your photographer probably has some thoughts about stage setup, backdrops or lighting.

Don't undervalue the knowledge, skills and experiences of the other people invested in your event's success. Most of them want to see you succeed because they look good when you do. Their success reflects well on you and yours on them. These win-win relationships are more valuable than you may realize.

When vendors see you as someone who prioritizes collaboration, communicates well and is easy to work with, they'll give you glowing recommendations and refer you to other great people so that everyone continues to win.

Microphone Control

Taking charge of the microphone as the event emcee means giving up control of the behind-the-scenes run of the show. You might not be ready for that yet. Remember that if your mind is somewhere else when you're on stage to talk to your guests, they'll sense it. When you choose to step onto your own stage as the host plus emcee, you answer to your audience. Your job is to meet and exceed their expectations of you and your event. They need to know they can count on you. They need to know that you're present with them. They need to know that they are the most important people in the room.

It's not about the script. It's not about what time it is. It's not about whether the tech is working or not. Stay present and be yourself. If you have the bandwidth and energy to serve your audience as their emcee, and you can have some fun while doing it, keep doing it!

On the other hand, if you're feeling overwhelmed by all the different aspects of emceeing that go into a successful production, prefer to hang out behind the curtain or realize that your time is more effectively spent elsewhere in the long list of event hosting duties above, it might be the right time to outsource control of the microphone.

14

THE PROFESSIONAL EMCEE EDGE

"Good is not good when better is expected."
— Vin Scully

A LOT OF HOSTS don't think about the value of working with a professional emcee until it's too late. Their go-to volunteer emcee is suddenly unavailable. Their first-choice emcee is booked, and so is their second and third choice. Their budget runs out before they get around to hiring an emcee, and they can't afford the quality professional they really need. They end up with an okay event and a disappointed audience—even if politeness prevents people from saying so on the feedback form.

Your emcee is the conductor of your event—ensuring that everyone involved is playing the right notes at the right tempo in the right key. Most people don't give the emcee much thought, but when they're missing or downright unprofessional, it disrupts the harmony of the entire experience for everyone involved.

I've seen this happen firsthand as both a speaker and an attendee, and I'm not the only one. I want to share some real stories to demonstrate what a difference a professional emcee can make. The case studies included here come from different types of events with different goals and challenges, and they illustrate the point that the right emcee can transform an ordinary event into an extraordinary experience.

Case Study: Warrior Unchained

What happens when a passionate heart-centered entrepreneur creates an event from scratch, her own hands on every detail? What changes when she releases her vice grip on control and invites a professional emcee to share the responsibility?

Wendy Babcock wanted to attend an event that combined personal growth with professional training geared toward GenX women business owners. She couldn't find one, so she created her own conference in 2019 called *Warrior Unchained.*

In 2019, Wendy brought together incredible speakers and invited her network to attend. She told her own life-changing story from the stage for the first time and deeply connected with her guests. In turn, they deeply connected with each other. Even though the event lost money, it struck a chord with her clientele and made a lasting impact on the lives of the people in attendance. With time to reflect and plan during the 2020 pandemic, she brought back the event in 2022. This time, she enlisted the help of friends and family who volunteered to take pictures, handle registration and DJ, but Wendy was still doing most of the event management herself.

At *Warrior Unchained* 2022, a tech issue with the video capture made it so that Wendy couldn't deliver some of the value she had promised to her speakers. She was devastated, even though the speakers were gracious. Wendy also realized that as much of an impact her event had on the audience, she herself hadn't experienced even a fraction of the magic because she was so busy coordinating everything both on and off the stage. She introduced every speaker. She announced every break. She facilitated every activity. By the end of the event, she was mentally, emotionally and physically drained and unsure whether Warrior Unchained would return the next year.

In 2023, I approached Wendy to get on her stage and work with her as her emcee. She immediately felt her burden lift. With someone else running the show and facilitating transitions and activities, she could feel herself breathing easier even before the planning was in full swing.

When I sought out feedback after the event in September 2023, Wendy's husband thanked me for everything I did because it made a difference in her energy and enthusiasm for the event. Wendy herself told me, "For the first time, I was able to relax and actually enjoy my own event!" Wendy realized that despite being a highly accomplished international and TEDx speaker, emceeing requires a completely different skillset, which she had no interest in developing for herself once she realized how impactful it could be to collaborate with a professional.

Don't take it from me, here's Wendy's account in her own words:

> In 2019, I had a big idea—I wanted to host an event. Not just any event—I envisioned an empowerment event for women complete with massages, vendor booths, dancing, yoga, music, meals, speakers and even hula-hooping.
>
> And the best part? I had never hosted an event before. I had absolutely no idea what I was doing.
>
> Guess how it went?
>
> I did all the planning, booked the venue, chose the meals,

picked the speakers, made the slide decks, selected the music, created the schedule, designed the centerpieces and included all the extras I thought were necessary.

I also ran all the tech, handled the audio and emceed it.

It was amazing, fulfilling and I received so much praise! It also put me $4,000 in the hole and left me completely exhausted for at least a week afterward.

Then, in 2022, as the world started opening up again, I decided to host the event once more. This time, I was determined to be smarter about it. I cut back on all the unnecessary extras. Yet, I still did everything—planning, tech, audio—and emceed my own event.

Financially, I broke even. But once again, I was utterly drained and left questioning why I continued doing this, despite the rave reviews.

Then I got an email.

It was from a lovely woman who had attended the event at the invitation of a friend. She complimented me on the experience and said something that changed every-thing for me:

"In my feedback about the last event, I suggested that having an emcee to tie everything together would take Warrior to the next level for me as an attendee.

So my question is, what would it take for me to emcee Warrior 2023?"

Honestly, I had never considered bringing in an emcee before. The moment I read that email, though, I couldn't respond fast enough. I was intrigued.

I felt a sense of relief when I got that email from Sara. I had always felt like I was running around like a chicken with my head cut off at my own event. I barely had time to sit down before having to hop on stage again. While I love speaking, emceeing requires a different kind of energy—more pizazz, more presence, the ability to seamlessly introduce speakers, keep the event on schedule and direct the flow of energy throughout.

So, I took a leap of faith and brought Sara in as the emcee for the 2023 event.

The first thing I noticed? Suddenly, I had an ally. Someone who was excited to be part of the event, who truly listened and who understood what I was trying to accomplish.

Sara was right alongside me during the planning process, ensuring she knew the full event timeline. She personally reached out to speakers to get to know them beyond their bios. She checked in with me often, offering insights and suggestions and making sure I didn't feel like I had to carry everything alone. She even helped promote the event!

So, how did Warrior 2023 go with Sara as the emcee?

Not only did I turn a profit, for the first time, I got to sit down, relax and actually enjoy my event.

Who knew one person could make that big of a difference?

Naturally, I hired her again for the 2024 event, and it was the best one yet! Sara's preparation, confidence and ability to read and respond to the audience's energy were phenomenal.

For the first time, I didn't just run my event—I experienced it. I even participated in networking activities! It was also my most profitable event to date. Sara not only helped promote it, she also introduced key partners who came on as event sponsors.

Listen, I get it. It's possible to DIY an event, power through and "get it done." But take it from me—having an emcee made all the difference.

— Wendy Babcock, Event Host

Case Study: The Longest Day

While multi-day conferences like Warrior Unchained can show the impact that bringing in a quality emcee can have on a large event, smaller gatherings can benefit just as much. When Ann Matuszak hosted a fundraiser for the Alzheimer's Association, she didn't think she needed an emcee until she realized that the value of the partnership went way beyond her bottom line!

Ann is known as The Photo Solutions Guru.[1] She helps people organize and preserve their memories—from photographs, videotapes and film negatives to obscure digital files and more. She is also passionate about supporting people who have loved ones with Alzheimer's disease.

In 2024, she created her own fundraiser for The Longest Day to benefit the Alzheimer's Association and called it, "Photos and Memories." The main activity of the event was for Ann to teach attendees how to effectively sort and organize their photographs. She spoke about how photographs can help people with memory loss because memories of photographs are stored in a different part of the brain than memories of the actual events.

Ann knew that her inaugural event would be on the smaller side, and she set a modest fundraising goal. On the day of the event, Ann and I showed up at the venue with our boxes of photographs—or in my case, a large suitcase! A handful of people stopped by and dropped off donations or photos for Ann. For the most part, though, the two of us spent the entire day sorting our own photos, chatting and listening to music.

Instead of focusing on how many people weren't there in person with us, I went live on Instagram to share what we were doing and why we were doing it. Even though we weren't the greatest with the tech on the fly, we were able to reach people online who wouldn't have otherwise known about the event. Ann met her fundraising goal, despite things not going entirely according to plan.

In Ann's words:

---

1. https://photosolutionsguru.com

Over my professional career, I have hosted dozens of events, and I really didn't think I needed an emcee. I like Sara, so I thought I would have her emcee my Longest Day event, which is a fundraiser for the Alzheimer's Association. After this event, I will never do an event without Sara as my emcee!

I ran into personal challenges before the event occurred, and Sara was promoting the event, being a cheerleader for it and putting out social media posts for me when I didn't have the capacity to do it myself. On the day of the event, I was kind of emotionally broken. Sara went live on social media and interviewed me. She played a huge part in keeping the event fun and moving.

I cannot overemphasize the value that Sara as the emcee brought to my event and I'm so looking forward to working with her again and again!
                        — Ann Matuszak, Photo Solutions Guru

In the Absence of a Pro

When you're paying attention—and if you've gotten this far in the book, I hope that you are—the value of a professional emcee can be felt the most when they're not in the room. I asked another professional emcee, Mitch Nelles, to share one of his experiences with me to illustrate how sometimes people learn the hard way.

I'm active with a certain nonprofit, and a couple of years ago, they had a situation. The executive director likes to do the live auction, and he's actually decent at it—not the best, and he has a bit of an ego about it, but he does a nice job.

One year, he fell seriously ill just before their event.

I wasn't scheduled to attend that year, but I've probably been to this event at least five different times. I've been on the board, and I'm very active with the mission and the day-to-day operations.

The chair of the board did the auction, and it was a disaster. He had no idea what he was doing, and it devolved into a pretty uncomfortable situation.

The chair-elect, a good friend of mine, called me immediately afterward and apologized for not calling me. Their numbers were way down, and if they had called in a professional—I would have done it—it would have been a resounding success.
     — Mitch Nelles, Professional Emcee & Radio Host

Beyond Conferences

It's not only conferences that experience the challenges of hosts wearing too many hats. All kinds of events can benefit from having a skilled emcee taking the lead. Andie Miller spent years producing dance events while juggling both production and emceeing duties.

For 15 years, I was a dance teacher and troupe director of an adult dance troupe. Every year for eleven of those years, I hosted a dance showcase for the troupe to display their talents to their friends and families.

While it started small, it eventually grew into a full day event with workshops taught by a guest instructor during the day and a formal showcase in the evening at a local high school theater. We had stage lighting, professional sound engineering, regional guest performers, plus our headliner.

While each of these elements enhanced the experience for both the dancers and the audience, they were also potential issues for me as the event organizer to deal with on the day of the event.

I often had to compose myself enough to calmly go on stage and explain to the audience why we were starting late, why we were taking a brief 5 minute break or why the dancers would be performing out of the order listed in the program, all the while trying to convince the audience members to be patient and stay in their seats so we wouldn't have them interrupting the performance.

I also needed to give the "welcome" speech at the beginning of the show, remember to say all the important reminders (silence your cell phones, no flash photography, don't block the videographer's camera, etc.) while being very aware of the timing—is the first act ready to go once I'm done? Are all my dancers fully ready? Am I fully ready? What's the choreography for the opening number again...?

I always forgot something!

Imagine if I had a professional emcee to welcome the audience while I was backstage with my dancers giving them a last minute pep talk or to explain any delays to the audience and keep them entertained with their "butts in the seats." That would have been a huge relief for me. It would have allowed me to quickly take care of the issues behind the scenes, shortening the delay or even allowing me to be more present in the moment to enjoy the show.

— Zhara Sagira, Dance Instructor

Partner for Growth

There are many reasons for an entrepreneur to start hosting events. When you're putting together your first, second or third conference or big event, there is a lot to learn. As you begin to gain confidence in the event space and as your audience begins to grow, you start to look for ways to improve the experience. You streamline your processes and increase the value for your guests.

As a professional emcee, I see myself as a member of your growth team, a strategic partner through all phases from prep to post. When a host brings me on board, I become their biggest fan. I do whatever it takes to make sure that everyone involved has a phenomenal experience. I make it my mission to help the hosts reach their goals or beyond, make the speakers look brilliant and give the audience a transformational and enjoyable experience while we're together. I want everyone to rave about your event and enthusiastically return year after year.

A professional emcee isn't just a pretty face who gets some laughs and tells you where the restroom is. Your emcee can be the reason that tens of thousands of dollars pour into your event, cause or organization...or not.

15

CO-CREATIVE
COLLABORATION

"Collaboration is like carbonation for fresh ideas.
Working together bubbles up ideas you would not
have come up with solo, which gets you further faster."

— Caroline Ghosn

M Y FIRST JOB WAS slinging concessions at a local six-screen
cinema. I waited tables in college. I was a bookseller at
a national chain bookstore after graduating with a fancy liberal
arts degree. I've cared for children and edited books and designed
websites. I've attempted network marketing and online sales. I've
taught childbirth education and martial arts classes. I've been a
professional handwriter, a postpartum doula and an actor. I've
been a camp counselor and a coach. I've always been artistic and
creative in expressing myself, and I've always had a heart to help
people, regardless of my job description.

I did not realize that emceeing was my true zone of genius until
the middle of my life. I spent a lot of time discovering who I
am and building skills on top of my natural talents and abilities.
There are many emcees who have spent years specializing and
focusing on learning the art of public speaking and developing
their professional emceeing skills. I'm more of a jack-of-all-trades
type, which I actually consider an asset because knowing a little
bit about a lot of things helps me to bring a broad perspective to

life and business. One of my greatest strengths is connecting the dots and seeing patterns where others don't. I credit this to my wide range of interests and varied experiences.

You cannot produce an event entirely on your own, even if you feel like you're the only one who can or will do what needs to be done. If there's one thing that I hope I've hammered into you throughout this book, it's the fact that people are the most important part of your event (including you). I've been in situations where I felt I was entirely on my own, and it sucks. I don't recommend it. Surround yourself with people who can help you create an incredible experience, and your load will lighten. Your vision will expand as well as your energy, impact and reach.

The Wish List

Most of us move through the world with expectations bouncing around in our subconscious minds. We hardly notice them until we find ourselves disappointed when they go unmet. Most of us don't know what we expect from something or someone unless they disappoint us. The wish list is a helpful tool to identify your expectations. When you know what you want from the beginning, you reduce your chances of being disappointed in the end.

I hope that you take some time to create your delegation wish list. You can use a blank piece of paper or a notebook. You can record your voice or a video. You can tell a friend or business partner. You can make a spreadsheet, a collage or a diorama. It doesn't matter what form your wish list takes as long as you make one.

SIDE NOTE:

You can make a wish list for absolutely everything! I've made wish lists for the qualities I wanted in a best friend, types of networking connections and the perfect client. I have a wish list for how I want my house to look. I have one from when I was looking for the right job. I'm married, and I still made a wish list for what I wanted in an ideal husband. (I even got some of the items on that list after more than two decades with the same partner!) It works. For anything. Try it!

Write down no fewer than 20 answers to the question: *Given an unlimited budget for this event, what do you want?*

If you're feeling any resistance to this exercise or find yourself bumping up against concerns about how to make it all happen, the point isn't the how. It's not even to make your every wish come true. The point is to get you thinking bigger—beyond the limitations that won't be holding you back forever.

Think again about the vision you created for your event at the beginning. Now look at your wish list through the lens of your vision and goals. Which three items on your wish list are the most likely to help you to achieve your event's ideal outcome? That's what you should prioritize.

If an emcee didn't make your top three, we need to have words.

As someone with valuable connections, creativity and unique perspectives, your emcee sees what you don't. Your emcee reflects your vision back to you when you get lost in the details and lose sight of your larger purpose. A professional emcee is removed enough from your organization that they can ask simple questions without judgment and help you refine your event's mission even further.

A professional emcee is so much more than a pretty face behind a microphone.

Share your wish list and ideal outcomes with your emcee. That way, they're able to customize their performance to you and your organization in ways that you might not have thought about doing yourself. Emcees are also often very well connected and active in a variety of spaces, so if you find yourself in need of referrals or recommendations, your emcee can be a valuable resource, pointing you in the right direction or making personal introductions.

How I Work

When I'm hired to emcee an event, first I meet with the host and ask a LOT of questions. I ask about the vision and goals for the event, ideal outcomes, audience demographics, sponsors, speakers and anything else I want to know about their organization or origin story. As we have this conversation, I begin to think about the people in my world who might make good sponsors, speakers, vendors or audience members for their event.

On my own time, I thoroughly research the host and organization as well as any past events they've held. I do a deep dive and brainstorm different ways I might build on the good work that they've already done or plan to do. I consider how to make the event more of what it already is and imagine what it could be.

I schedule regular meetings with the event host(s) and continue to ask questions as they arise. I research the speakers, and depending on the level of my involvement, I reach out to connect with them directly. I also offer consultation and feedback on scripts, transitions, activities and the entire agenda.

I may create and customize an online collaborative photo album, if applicable. I show the host how to navigate the photo service and may create custom album cover images if requested. I create short links and QR codes so they can be easily added to print and digital promotional materials.

When the host gets overwhelmed or panics about anything related to the event, I'm on the phone, in their email box, text messages, on Zoom or Marco Polo offering empathy and practical support. I nudge them if they're taking too long to make a decision and celebrate with them when they land a presenting sponsor.

When I'm provided with a script, I rewrite it in my own voice so that when I'm speaking, I don't sound like I'm reading a script. I print the agenda, script, speaker introductions, announcements, sponsor information and any supplemental material onto note-cards. I practice reading all the words out loud several times on my own before rehearsal.

On the day of the event, I watch the host, the clock, the audience and the stage. I make it my mission to make sure that of all the things the host has to worry about during the course of the event, I am not one of them.

One of my personal goals as an emcee is for the host to enjoy the fruits of their labor and have some fun, too!

16

INVEST IN SUCCESS

"Price is what you pay. Value is what you get."
— Warren Buffett

I LOVE ATTENDING CONFERENCES. It's thrilling to gather with large groups of people who share common backgrounds or aspirations. I know how much work goes into producing big events, and you will never find me bad mouthing anyone's efforts in this arena. What I will often do is take note of amazing engagement activity ideas or moments that fall flat so that I can take that knowledge and improve my next performance.

At an industry conference I attended for my day job, I appreciated how engaging the speakers were and how the emcees (who were also members of the host organization as well as keynote speakers) guided the flow of activity from the stage. They knew the script. They knew the agenda. They did well keeping the event running on time. They were obviously experienced professional speakers. If you're going to host your own event, the way these two performed is something to strive for.

Through my professional emcee lens, though, something was off. I felt a lack of coherence. What was missing was a common thread tying each speaker to the larger theme of the conference. Because the emcees were also speakers themselves, their roles were not always as clear cut as they could have been. The line between their educational and transitional content blurred a few times. I also counted three different themes, and it didn't seem like all of the sponsors knew which theme was the most relevant to their offers.

These are all very minor issues, and they did not detract from the overall positive experience of the conference. However, leveraging the top-secret professional emcee skills I've shared in these pages could have significantly improved the entire experience.

When you hire a pro, you're bringing aboard an experienced captain to take charge of your ship, keep their eyes on the horizon and course correct as needed. You have someone for the audience, speakers and sponsors to look to for guidance and direction and someone to have your back when things go sideways. I don't mind being your scapegoat if I have to because my job is to make you look amazing.

Adding a professional emcee can make your "okay" event out of this world! Your audience will leave with their usual takeaways from the content PLUS they'll feel well cared for and connected throughout the process. They'll be eager to share their experience with others who weren't there and articulate it more effectively when they do.

The Cost

One emcee I saw (not a professional) got flustered when the audience wouldn't settle down after a break. Instead of using a strategy to bring the room back to their seats, the emcee gave the group a good scolding, like a teacher laying down the law in a classroom full of kindergarteners. During the break, I heard comments from some people that they didn't like the part where they "got yelled at" by the emcee to sit down and shut up so they could listen to yet another sponsor sell them something.

A colleague of mine was a keynote speaker at another conference where the emcee, an industry big wig, board member or manager of some sort, got more and more drunk throughout the event. Visibly. If your emcee needs alcoholic lubrication to speak in front of a crowd, you might want to consider an alternative.

Think about the funds you *don't raise* because of your novice auctioneer.

Think about the presenting sponsor who *doesn't return* next year because you forgot to thank them.

Think about the *migraine you'll get* halfway through your event because you're juggling too much and pushing yourself too hard.

The right emcee for your event should bring their A game from start to finish, from prep to post. They know that they represent your brand, your mission and your vision for the duration. They know that their job requires more than showing up and reading a script. They know how to connect to people on an authentic human level to encourage deeper contemplation and inspire action. They know how to manage their own energy and the energy of the room. Emceeing is a big job, and not everyone is suited for it.

If you're hosting a day-long or multi-day conference, you're already investing a ton of time, money and energy on the planning and production side of things. You want the performance to be as exciting for the audience as it has been for you to produce. To take it to the next level, I highly recommend investing in a high quality professional emcee.

You can use all the tools in the book and be good *enough* to do it yourself. And I'll be so proud of you for taking the role seriously and getting it done! If emceeing is an afterthought, though, or it's not your passion or within your current skillset, you don't have to do it. You can outsource the job, and I'll show you how.

How to Find and Hire Your High ROI Emcee

The difference between an average event and an awesome one shows up in your bottom line. Your investment in a quality emcee can pay for itself and more. For example:

- Increased sponsorship revenue from attraction and retention efforts

- Increased per-person fundraising donations

- Larger percentage of donor participation

- Engaged attendees becoming repeat ticket buyers and word-of-mouth promoters

- Increased long-term revenue for host organizations and sponsor companies from amplified brand awareness

- Access to new professional networks for event marketing, promotion and collaboration opportunities

- Preservation of the host's time and energy

- Longevity and sustainability resulting from the host's increased enjoyment of the experience

You can put a number on most of these bullet points, and a well-connected professional can hook you up with incredible speakers, generous sponsors and enthusiastic, action-taking audiences. While the last two points don't necessarily translate into a clear dollar amount, your ability to find enjoyment, ease and flow as you plan and execute your event can make a huge difference in the quality of your own experience as well as your willingness to do it again.

While my clients have enjoyed the financial ROI from working with me, the feedback I value most from them is when they express the more intangible rewards, like enjoyment, freedom and relief. You may not realize the value of sharing the mental load until you experience it for yourself, which is why selecting an emcee who has your back in more than one way is so impactful.

When you consider your options for who will emcee your event, think about people who are already in your circle. Who has the kind of vibe and energy that would fit in with your event? Have they spoken in front of a crowd of people before? Do they have the skills we've been discussing throughout this book? Are they easy for you to work with? Do they communicate clearly and openly? Are they willing to offer you feedback or will they withhold valuable information from you in order to keep the peace? Are they confident enough to command the stage and generous enough to share it?

If someone comes to mind immediately, and they are not a professional emcee (yet), determine a reasonable offer in exchange for their services. You know your budget, and sometimes a barter arrangement is entirely appropriate. If they are a professional emcee who is already speaking as part of their business, pay them. Make them a real money offer. If their full fee is not within your budget, be upfront and offer what you can. Sweeten the deal with creative ways to compensate them to show them you understand and appreciate the value they add to your event.

If you don't have anyone in mind, ask the people in your circle for recommendations. When your friends have worked with someone successfully, they're usually more than happy to make a recommendation.

Finally, if your network doesn't come through for you, you can continue your search on Google, GigSalad or other speaker websites. You can find Facebook groups full of speakers or search local or national speaking agencies.

Once you've narrowed your search to 3-5 emcees, it's time to interview them. Set up a connection call and have your interview questions ready. (You can download your 13 Questions to ask your emcee PDF for free from welcometothestagebook.com/resourc es.)

After the interviews, you should have a good sense of which of your finalists would fit best with your event vision. Feel free to reach out to your top choices with any follow-up or clarifying questions.

Once you sign a contract and pay their fee, USE YOUR EMCEE!

So many times, I've seen hosts hire an emcee and completely forget that they exist. Your emcee wants to serve you and make your event unbelievable! If I'm working with you, I want to work with you! Your emcee is there to advance your mission, your goal, your audience and your sponsors. If you don't tap into the resources they have made available to you, it's your loss.

As a professional emcee client, you enter into an essential partnership. Even though in the early stages of your event, the investment may seem like an optional luxury, I hope that you've learned how much really goes into a smooth performance and either take the time to do the job well yourself or collaborate with someone who fits your vision.

I promise that investing in your emcee—whether it's training one of your own or hiring out a pro—will be well worth it!

CONCLUSION

YOUR ROLE, YOUR CHOICE

THANK YOU AND GOOD NIGHT

"People will forget what you said, people will forget what you did, but people will never forget how you made them feel."

— Maya Angelou

A GOOD EMCEE CLOSES the show by reinforcing the theme, reminding the audience of some key takeaways or memorable moments and sending them off with some heartfelt words and a simple action step to take as they leave.

There's a reason that you had the idea for your event. It's part of your purpose, and it can make a real difference for people in the world. You are creative and brilliant, and there are so many people who will benefit from your efforts. Your event is something that only you can produce. In a disconnected world, your event can bring people together for good—to heal, to grow, to share, to align, to ignite, to imagine, to excel, to inspire, to empower.

In part one, we discussed why your event matters. You filtered your event's main focus through the five C's: cash, credibility, clients, community and collaboration. You learned why and how your business benefits from hosting events. I invited you to take a closer look at the emcee role and how it can expand beyond the common assumptions and increase your impact. We walked through a dreaming process to design your ideal event.

In part two, we covered what makes a great event. You learned more about the role of the emcee, the importance of people and how to lead from the stage. I gave you three keys to confidence (practice, practice, practice) and suggested some different ways to highlight your credibility, authority and authenticity by developing your stage presence and having fun at the same time.

In part three, we dove deeper into taking the stage and the technical aspects of running the show. We went over the art and science of reading a room. I shared some tools and techniques that make engagement easy.

In part four, I made the case for a professional emcee, sharing some real-life experiences from clients and colleagues to highlight the benefits of bringing in a professional. We talked about what's at stake when your emcee is an afterthought.

My intention with this book has been to equip you as much as possible to be successful as an emcee even if it's not your calling or passion and to emphasize the value of filling the role with a skilled professional when you're ready to invest in one. The right emcee can bring their expertise and experience from outside your organization and help you create the kind of event experiences you didn't realize were missing.

You're busy. We all are. We're all looking for ways to maximize our productivity and outsource the activities that drain us. If standing on a stage, thinking on your feet, co-creating an epic experience with an audience of individuals and cheerleading for speakers and sponsors isn't quite your thing, start a conversation with someone like me who loves doing all of it.

I'm happy to connect with you and help you make your event amazing. If you have questions or any trouble implementing the ideas in this book, reach out to me. If you think I would make a great emcee for your next event, let's talk about working together. If not, that's cool, too. I know I'm not the only amazing emcee in the world, and if there's anything I can do to help you find or develop the right emcee for you, let me know.

You can connect with me at saradeacon.com. I'd love to hear from you!

Acknowledgments

This book wouldn't have been possible without the support of so many people.

First and foremost, I want to thank my husband, James. He picked up a lot of the responsibilities I dropped as I focused my efforts on these pages and cheered me on every step of the way. Not every badass woman has a partner like this in her corner, so I never want to take him for granted. I appreciate him more than he knows.

I have to give a shout out to my sons, Michael, Andrew and Daniel. With everything I do I hope to provide them with an example of what a strong woman looks like and what it might look like for them to follow their dreams, creativity and passions for themselves. I want to thank them for being exactly who they are and for the occasional interruptions asking me for a hug when I didn't realize it was exactly what I needed.

I wouldn't be here without Wendy Babcock. She brought out the speaker in me and trusted me to emcee her event when all I had was the vague idea that I could do it. She handed me the microphone, and we have both been transformed because of the friendship that followed. She's a magical human, and everyone should know her name. If you have a story that needs to be told, talk to Wendy.

For helping me find my voice, I want to thank all of my networking groups and all of the brilliant minds who have shared their wisdom through Defining Leaders, PONG, Business Over Breakfast, Young Guns, Rely Local, several different Chambers of Commerce, Hopportunity Networking, Milwaukee Breakfast Club, PWOW, Small Business Milwaukee Think Tank, Cre8tive Con, Breakfast with Champions and the Small Business Owners Community. These are incredibly welcoming groups of individuals who genuinely want to help one another grow their businesses. I wouldn't be where I am today without them.

So many individuals I consider to be my "business besties" have had my back through more than one big challenge over the last few years. They have gone above and beyond the call of duty and held space for so many ups and downs. There are too many of them to name here, and I wouldn't want to unintentionally leave anyone out. I promise to go out of my way to share my appreciation and gratitude with them directly as often as possible.

I asked many people to share their experiences with me for this book, and I appreciate all of the contributors including Wendy, Mitch, Andie, Ann and those who indirectly offered insight via social media posts, candid conversations and my silly polls.

Thank you to Connect Chiropractic for keeping me aligned in more ways than one. I'm not sure where I would be without such a healing work environment and the steady paycheck that relieved a lot of pressure from my life and business.

Finally, my parents have believed in me 100% since the very beginning. They have provided me with positive examples, advice, encouragement and practical support throughout my life, and they've been my biggest fans in every endeavor I've chosen to pursue. They have given me so much more than they know, and I am beyond grateful for all the tangible and intangible ways they have loved me over the years.

About the author

Sara Deacon is a creative force who brings magic to every event she touches. With a knack for turning ordinary moments into extraordinary experiences, her expertise as a professional emcee, award-winning speaker and accomplished author helps her to connect with and inspire others beyond all expectations.

A skillful master of ceremonies who brings humor and authenticity to the stage, Sara has the rare ability to light up a room and make everyone feel seen and heard. Whether she's facilitating conversations at a large conference, creating her own content or polishing anthologies and coordinating production events for WHEN Stories™, Sara makes sure that every piece fits together just right.

With advanced degrees in English and Creative Writing, her journey as a writer and editor gives her a storytelling edge, helping her craft narratives that resonate with a wide range of audiences, making her a driving force behind impactful events and publications alike.

When she's not holding a microphone or playing with words, Sara loves connecting deeply with people who are passionate about their own purpose. With Sara in the room, you'll rise to the next challenge, knowing you have a genuine cheerleader and supporter in your corner.

Connect with Sara at saradeacon.com.